Quest for Lancelot's Arthur

QUEST FOR LANCELOT'S ARTHUR

RESEARCHING LANCELOT'S GRAIL BY TOURING KING ARTHUR'S BRITAIN

RICHARD GARTEE

LAKE AND EMERALD PUBLICATIONS

Books by Richard Gartee
—Non-Fiction—
The Hippodrome Theatre First Fifty Years
Skating on Skim Ice
Quest for Lancelot's Arthur
—Fiction—
Lancelot's Grail
Lancelot's Disciple
Orgone Gizmo
Atlantis Dying
Atlantis Obsession
Ragtime Dudes at the World's Fair
Ragtime Dudes in a Thin Place
Ragtime Dudes Meet a Paris Flapper
—Poetry—
Mountain Breathing
Watching Waves
Canyon Falls
Arbor Encore

A complete list of currently available titles by the author can be found at www.gartee.com

Copyright © 2025 Richard Gartee
All rights reserved.

Published by Lake and Emerald Publications, LLC
Gainesville, FL

ISBN 978-1-7363957-9-0

Library of Congress Control Number: 2024910394

Unless otherwise credited all photos © Richard Gartee. Photos with † symbol are licensed from Adobe, Inc. Photos with ‡ symbol are licensed under terms of creative commons.org. For a complete list of credits including public domain figures, see pages 172–173.

Front piece and back cover: Stained glass panel of King Arthur and Sir Lancelot commissioned in 1862 from Morris, Marshall, Faulkner & Co. by Walter Dunlop for Harden Grange near Bingley Yorkshire.

for
Sir Thomas Malory
compiler of the legend

Contents

Chapter 1 Glasgow 1
Chapter 2 Glastonbury Tor 10
Chapter 3 Ley Lines and Glastonbury-ness 20
Chapter 4 Camelot 30
Chapter 5 Glastonbury Abbey 41
Chapter 6 The Abbot's Kitchen 53
Chapter 7 A Surprising Meditation 59
Chapter 8 Camlann and Tintagel 62
Chapter 9 St. Nectan's Waterfall 73
Chapter 10 Bodmin Moor 82
Chapter 11 Salisbury and Old Sarum 87
Chapter 12 Stonehenge 95
Chapter 13 Marlborough 103
Chapter 14 Reflecting on the King 112
Chapter 15 A Dearth of Dark-Age Documents 116
Chapter 16 Enter the Knights 126
Chapter 17 Lancelot's Grail 135
Chapter 18 Sir Bedivere 140
Chapter 19 Percival 144
Chapter 20 Lancelot's Disciple 150
Chapter 21 Photographic References 156
Chapter 22 Myths and Bliss 168
Acknowledgments 171
About the Author 174

"If the deeds of an actual historical figure proclaim him to have been a hero, the builders of his legend will invent for him appropriate adventures in depth."

—*Joseph Campbell*

Chapter 1
Glasgow

"What is the purpose of your visit?" asked the immigration officer, a diminutive woman in a navy-blue uniform who spoke with a thick brogue.

I was standing in the airport terminal in Glasgow, Scotland, on my way to England to research background information for my novel, *Lancelot's Grail*. I didn't want to use the word "work" because saying work to an immigration officer anywhere in the world raises a whole set of issues you don't want to get into.

"Well, I'm interested in King Arthur. I'm going to tour around Britain."

"But why did you come *here*?"

I looked at her, completely befuddled. "Because this is where the plane landed?"

I could have said, "Because I'm cheap, and my travel agent found a fly-by-night airline with a convoluted route that connected through three cities and had a long layover." But I didn't. Since I'd flown all night and had a six hour wait before my next flight, I just wanted to collect my bag from customs and recuperate before the next leg of my journey.

The Glasgow immigration officer gave me a puzzled look, shook her head, stamped my passport, and sent me on my way.

As I retrieved my carry-on bag, I realized she probably meant, why, if I was looking for King Arthur, did I come to Scotland? He wasn't Scottish.

By then, it was too late to correct my answer. But I sometimes replay, revise, or continue conversations in my mind long after they've ended. That was the case here.

I extended the handle on my suitcase and pulled it behind me through the terminal and out the sliding doors. The September sun felt warm, but the brisk breeze had a bite of cold. I was glad to be wearing my winter coat, although that probably hadn't helped mitigate the immigration officer's suspicions. My white, down-filled parka had a half-dozen large pockets, which I'd stuffed completely full, making me look like a lumpy polar bear or someone who should be frisked.

I am a fairly experienced traveler who learned years ago to never check my bag. I carry a regulation-size Rollaboard and cram it as full as possible. In addition, passengers can bring a small personal item, such as a laptop computer case, which I do. In it, I not only pack the laptop and its accessories but also my camera, headphones, phone charger, and a book. Early in my travels, I discovered that your coat or jacket doesn't count as luggage. So, when I have both bags maxed-out, I take additional items in my jacket pockets. On this trip, my parka bulged with gloves, a scarf, my journal, a change of socks, bags of trail mix, dried fruit, and more.

Heavy? Yes. That normally isn't a concern because I just usually go from the plane to a taxi or car, and then to a hotel. In Glasgow, however, this wasn't the case. I had hours to kill, and I was sick of airports. The bargain-price ticket had required driving to Sanford, Florida, which is about three hours from my home, and checking in hours early for a ten p.m. flight. Sanford, a city less than half the size of Gainesville, where I live, had somehow gotten its airport designated as an international airport. Milling around the international terminal with hundreds of other passengers, I awaited our departure.

Night flights to Europe are exhausting, anyway. You already feel as if you've traveled a full day by the time you take off; and let no one

Chapter 1 Glasgow

convince you that you can get any quality sleep during an overnight flight. To make matters worse, my plane first flew to Belfast, Northern Ireland, a stopover I didn't know about when I booked the trip. In Belfast, passengers continuing to Scotland had to stay aboard, but I couldn't sleep with departing passengers opening and closing overhead bins and flight attendants moving up and down the aisles. After an hour or two on the ground in Belfast, we proceeded to Glasgow.

After extended hours of plane travel, fatigue becomes superseded by that type of hyper sleeplessness similar to that of kids who get exhausted but won't go to bed. Besides, airports have nowhere comfortable to sleep. So, I pulled my wheeled-suitcase to a bus stop, and took a local bus to city centre. Glasgow residents walked about in shirtsleeves, but as a Floridian, anything below sixty degrees feels like winter to me. Of course, I didn't know the actual temperature. The UK measures in Celsius and I was too mentally fatigued to do the math conversion, so I just kept my parka on.

The first point of business was food. Airplane meals, when they exist at all, are insubstantial and meaningless. Airport food is worse. I'd subsisted on dried fruit, trail mix, and airline pretzels on the flight over. My last real meal had been before I left for the Sanford airport over twenty hours earlier. I wanted something decent.

My wheeled bag and I roamed the Glasgow business district until I spotted Bella Italia. Yes, that's right—an Italian restaurant in the land of haggis.

I wasn't that surprised. I've found that major European cities have a diverse mix of ethnic restaurants, just like larger cities in the United States.

I am a vegetarian, and though European cities often have vegetarian restaurants somewhere, I had too much baggage and not enough time to schlep all over Glasgow searching for one. It has been my experience that Italian restaurants often have meatless pasta dishes on their menus. This one didn't, but I explained to my helpful Scottish server that I was a vegetarian, and she suggested a dish the chef could make without meat. I added a salad and a glass of red wine to my order.

While I waited, I made notes in my journal. The idea for the novel I was writing had come to me one weekend several years earlier, when a PBS show drew my attention to the fate of Lancelot after the fall of Camelot. Scorned and rejected by his once adoring public, he was sent away by his lover, Guinevere, to become a hermit monk. Yet the miraculous phenomena reported about him in his final months paralleled that experienced by yogis who had attained high states of enlightenment. What if, after years of questing for the Holy Grail, he'd found it during his isolation and solitude?

Throughout the previous decades, I'd had a strong interest in New Age teachings, Christian saints, Tibetan lamas, and Indian yogis. I had met and spent time with many remarkable spiritual teachers. Lancelot's situation seemed like the perfect framework for writing about some of the things I'd learned from the teachers I had encountered.

This, then, became the starting point for my novel. A famous man, known far and wide as the greatest knight, discovers the path to enlightenment while living in isolation. I asked myself, if during his seclusion Lancelot had at last found the Grail and achieved a mystical state, what of his discovery was he obligated to share, and with whom? And how would he accomplish this in his isolation?

My story's protagonists are Alura and Frith, a sister and brother who were abandoned at an abbey as children. They are now grown up and desperate for a new life. After they discover Lancelot's hermitage in a forest behind the abbey, he tutors them on how to penetrate the barriers within that keep them from attaining the Grail. In the process, Lancelot expounds upon various ideas I'd uncovered during my own quest.

Once I completed a couple of drafts, I decided to visit Britain to gather authentic details that would enhance my novel. While there are no known historical locations associated with Lancelot, he spent a great deal of time with King Arthur, whose sites are well known in Britain. So, this was my plan: fly to England, rent a car, and visit every historical

Chapter 1 Glasgow

or archeological site associated with King Arthur. In theory, by walking through these places, I could sense or infer what Lancelot saw.

Now, I was, only hours away from Bristol, my jumping off point. Not that Bristol was in any way connected to King Arthur, but it was the closest major airport to places where he had lived and breathed. Choosing Bristol also let me avoid flying into London, where I'd landed on previous trips. London traffic is a mess, and from there I would have required a full day to drive to Cornwall and southwest Britain, the area I wanted to explore.

Figure 1-1 Bella Italia restaurant in Glasgow.

My server brought my dinner, penne pasta baked in a rich tomato sauce and smothered with cheese, and a basket of warm bread. It smelled delicious, and the wine complimented the dish perfectly. I wanted to savor every bite, but I ate like a man who hadn't had a meal in twenty hours.

After eating, I checked the time. I still had hours before I needed to be back at the airport. I'd never been to Glasgow, so why not explore a bit? The city centre area charmed me with turreted brick buildings,

Art Nouveau architecture, and a large Victorian train station. A busker wearing a kilt played bagpipes on a street corner, and further up the street, I saw the Glasgow Kilt Company store. How authentic.

Figure 1-2 Busker in kilt playing bagpipes.

Chapter 1 Glasgow

Glasgow is home to the Scottish Opera, Scottish Ballet, and National Theatre of Scotland as well as acclaimed museums and the Royal School of Art, Music and Dance. I walked through this culturally rich area of town with my luggage in tow. Okay, the downside of not checking your bag is that you have to keep it with you between flights. That doesn't lend itself to sightseeing.

I made my way back to the bus stop and returned to the airport for my flight to Bristol. At check-in, I learned the maximum size for carry-on bags in Europe is about an inch smaller than the American standard, and a stubborn gate agent wouldn't let mine go on board with me, even after I pointed out that I'd just come off a plane in which it *was* allowed. "Yes," she explained, "but that flight originated in the United States, so it allowed United States-sized bags. The flight you're about to board originates here and must follow European size limits." In a compromise, she gate-checked it, meaning I'd get it back as soon as we deplaned and wouldn't have to hassle with baggage claim.

Upon landing in Bristol, I learned that the same airline also flew to Bristol from Belfast. Had I known when booking my ticket, I could have connected in Belfast and skipped the layover in Glasgow. On the other hand, I'd have missed the opportunity to see Glasgow.

I'd known I'd be arriving late after a full night and day of travel, so I did two things stateside to make my arrival in Britain go smoothly. I pre-booked my accommodation for the first night, so I could go straight to the hotel and fall asleep. Second, I'd rented a car from Hertz and pre-paid for it in America.

Getting the rental car was no problem with everything pre-arranged. The car was a tiny Ford. The smallest car I'd ever seen—as short as my living room sofa. Think of a loveseat on wheels. But this turned out to be a blessing. Many of the two-lane English country roads seemed no wider than an alley, lined on both sides with hedges that were taller than the car and grew right up to the road's edge. When English lorries, trucks about the size of a twenty-foot U-Haul, came barreling toward me, there was no place to go. I can't count the number of times I felt grateful to be driving the smallest car Hertz rented.

Figure 1-3 My rental car—the smallest Ford I'd ever seen.

The hotel was another issue. I told the nice chap at Hertz the address I needed to find, and he made a black and white Xerox of a map for me. It turned out my hotel, which I'd thought was in Bristol, was actually in Yatton, fourteen miles away on dark and winding roads. I had difficulty finding the hotel from the poor Xerox copy the rental agent gave me.

After passing its driveway several times, I finally found the place around 9:30 that night. When I entered the inn, I discovered a wedding reception in progress. I checked into my room and realized I was very hungry. I hadn't eaten since the meal in Glasgow seven hours earlier. Although I was exhausted from travel, hunger won. I went to the pub attached to the hotel and ate.

By the time I returned to my room, I was wiped-out. I had traveled for a long time, with only brief bouts of sleep on the plane. The wedding revelers stayed at it until 1:30 in the morning, and though I tried to sleep, they kept waking me. Once I finally got to sleep, I slept soundly until housekeeping knocked persistently on my door. I yelled, "I am still sleeping!"

The housekeepers answered back that they had to get the room ready for the next guests.

Chapter 1 Glasgow

Checkout time wasn't until ten-thirty or eleven. "What time is it?"

"12:20," the voice on the other side of the door answered.

Shocked, contrite, and groggy, I quickly showered, dressed, threw everything in my bag, and left, apologizing to the housekeepers waiting in the hall.

I had missed the free breakfast. So, I locked my luggage in the car and went to the pub to buy something to eat. The coffee was awful but necessary in my state. Having made three previous trips to England and traveled all over the UK, I've determined that you can't buy a decent cup of coffee in Britain. Café Americano is usually just water added to a shot of espresso, or worse, a bit of powdered coffee. Once, I did stay in a bed-and-breakfast that made coffee in a French press. That was good. On the other hand, the British claim they can't get a decent cup of tea in American restaurants. So maybe it's a trade-treaty or something. They won't compete with our coffee if we don't make tea the way they do. Or maybe they're still holding a grudge over the Boston Tea Party.

Still fatigued, I studied the map over breakfast. I decided to go straight to Glastonbury, as half the day was already gone and it was the closest of my planned stops.

Chapter 2
Glastonbury Tor

I motored to Glastonbury through winding back roads, parked the car on the street, and strolled around a town reminiscent of a hippie enclave from the late 1960s. All manner of New Age shops featured crystals, astrology paraphernalia, and tarot cards. King Arthur, the Round Table knights, Avalon, Celtic goddesses and fairies also had strong representation in local stores.

Since I'd made such a late start from Bristol and the afternoon was already aging, I decided to secure lodging for the night before touring the area. After inquiring at a couple of places without vacancies and another that wanted too much money, I walked back to the car to drop off my coat and some items I didn't want to carry. Then I locked the car and took a shortcut across a large public parking lot. That was fortuitous. A brick wall defined the back edge of the lot. A gate in the wall had a large daisy painted on it and a sign that said, "Accommodations Available." I pushed through and found myself in a charming garden where I met Daisy Foss, the proprietor. She showed me a clean, bright room on the ground floor, with its own entrance so I could come and go at will. I took it.

The Daisy Centre had a good vibe. It was a spiritual center focused on angels, who Daisy said had led her to buy the place. She held retreats, offered Reiki treatments, and hosted meditations there. She'd published a book, *Angels of Awakening: Lessons in Love, Life & Creation*, and said there was a copy of it in my room. I said I'd read it later.

CHAPTER 2 GLASTONBURY TOR

Figure 2-1 Daisy Centre exterior.

I moved my car from the street into the car park and found a space near Daisy's gate. I carried in my luggage, unpacked, and then left to do a little sightseeing before dark. Glastonbury is very touristy, but the town has two important sites, Glastonbury Abbey and Glastonbury Tor, both operated by the National Trust, the UK's large charity for the preservation of historic sites. Since I didn't want to be rushed while I visited the abbey, I elected to save that for the next day and visited only the tor that afternoon. The tor, a high hill visible from town, was a mile away. A shuttle bus transports tourists to and from there for one pound.

I walked down to the abbey parking lot and took the shuttle. The bus dropped me off at the base of the hill, from which I climbed a long, mostly paved path to the top. There, a three-story stone tower has stood for over a millennium; it was once part of St. Michael's Church.

Figure 2-2 Three-story St. Michael's Tower atop Glastonbury Tor.

The tower's exterior had corner buttresses, perpendicular bell openings, and seven canopied niches in the west face. Below the parapet was a

Figure 2-3 Inside view of St. Michael's Tower.

sculpted tablet with an image of an eagle. There were also carved reliefs over a deeply molded west door.

I entered the tower through a wide archway, and saw a matching archway on the opposite side. Inside were stone benches and an informational plaque about Glastonbury Tor and St. Michael's Tower. Looking up, I could see out the top as the tower was missing its upper stories and roof. In what must have been the upper floors, I spotted the battlements and bell openings I'd seen from outside.

I read the plaque and learned that the tower was not the Glastonbury Tor; I had incorrectly assumed it was due to the sound of the word. Actually, the tor is the entire conical-shaped hill. Its name is derived from the Old English word "torr," meaning a high rock or a hill.

This tor's sides have seven deep, roughly symmetrical terraces. These may have formed naturally by differentiation of clay and Lias stone layers, or they might be manmade defensive ramparts.

Another possibility for the tor's seven terraces is that medieval farmers terraced the hill for agricultural use to make plowing easier, or hooves of grazing cattle created the flattened paths. Even today, sheep and cows graze the tor, keeping the grass short in a natural and traditional way.

In line with Glastonbury's inclination toward the mystical, some people theorize that the terraces are a medieval spiritual walkway that was created for pilgrims, or the terraces are the remains of a three-dimensional labyrinth that originated during the Neolithic era.

From the top of the hill, I had a good view of the countryside and the town of Glastonbury below. At a height of 521 feet, Glastonbury Tor is a landmark for miles around. The view at the top of the conical hill encompasses the nearby village of Wells, the Quantock Hills, the Mendip Hills, peat moors rolling out to sea, and, some claim—on a clear day—even mountains in Wales. However, the day was pretty darn clear, yet I didn't see any mountains.

I reclined on the grassy hill below the tower, relaxing in the warm afternoon sun. Sheep grazed in the distance. Many places in Britain have a sense of ancient roots, and this was certainly one of them.

Chapter 2 Glastonbury Tor

Figure 2-4 The tor's terraced sides.

Neolithic flint tools recovered from the top of the Tor show that the site has been visited and occupied since prehistory. Nearby, the remains of Glastonbury Lake Village confirm that an Iron Age settlement existed there in about 300 or 200 BCE. Archeological finds, including Roman pottery, suggest that it was visited on a regular basis.

A couple of thousand years ago, a shallow sea reached inland to the base of Glastonbury Tor, nearly encircling it. The sea gradually receded, turning into freshwater wetlands and a vast lake. From most angles of approach, the tor would have appeared to be an island, and the old Celtic name for Glastonbury, Ynys-witrin, means "Island of Glass." Another name for Glastonbury Tor, perhaps more recognizable to modern readers, is the Isle of Avalon, named for the Celtic demigod Avalloc or Avallach, ruler of the underworld, who was believed to dwell there. According to Celtic lore, Avalon was the point where the dead passed to another level of existence. It was considered an enchanted isle—home to fairy folk.

The isle is technically a peninsula created by the River Brue flowing on three sides. The damp, low-lying ground can produce a visual effect known as a Fata Morgana, which causes the tor to appear to rise out

Figure 2-5 Fata Morgana effect surrounding the tor.

of the mist. This optical phenomenon occurs because rays of light are strongly bent when they pass through layers of air with different temperatures in a steep thermal inversion where an atmospheric duct has formed. Even though scientists explained away the mythical fairy home, they named the effect after Morgan le Fay, a powerful sorceress in Arthurian legend.

I admit my ignorance. When I'd boarded the bus an hour before, I had no idea the Tor was the Isle of Avalon. Although my mission was to visit sites said to have a connection with King Arthur, I had come to the Tor merely to see something local in what was left of the afternoon. I'd planned to dive into Arthur's world the following day. Yet learning this hilltop was Avalon meant I'd already begun, quite by accident. For this is where Arthur's life ended.

King Arthur's final battle was against Mordred, who was either his estranged son or nephew. In the battle, Arthur slew Mordred, but he was himself badly wounded. He repaired to Avalon, where he languished for some time and then eventually died.

As I looked around me, it felt increasingly likely that this site was the place where Arthur came to die. Certainly, a person in Arthur's time would have been influenced by the Tor's legend as a mystical place to ensure one's transition at death. But it was also strategic—high ground with terraced fortifications, exactly the type of place an experienced warrior would choose to recover after a devastating battle. In addition, the graves of King Arthur and Queen Guinevere had been found at an abbey only a mile from there.

Of course, Arthur wouldn't have seen the tower that now stood behind me. He died around 540 CE, but St. Michael's Monastery on Glastonbury Tor wasn't constructed until sometime between 900 and 1100 CE. That's not to say there weren't structures of some sort. Excavations on Glastonbury Tor between 1964 and 1966 revealed evidence of Dark Ages occupation from the fifth to the seventh centuries. Finds included postholes, two hearths, a metalworker's forge, two burials oriented north-south, fragments from sixth century Mediterranean amphorae used for wine or oil, and a worn hollow bronze head that may have once topped a Saxon staff.

I learned that during the late Saxon and early medieval periods at least four buildings stood on the summit. The base of a stone cross demonstrates Christian use of the site during this period when it perhaps served as a hermitage. The broken head of a wheel cross, found partway down the hill, and dated to the tenth or eleventh century may have been the top of the cross that stood on the summit.

The monastery and church on Glastonbury Tor were named for and dedicated to the Archangel St. Michael. Although all the buildings have disappeared, except for the tower, the existence of a monastic community on the tor is confirmed by a charter of 1243 granting permission for a fair to be held at the Monastery of St. Michael. Additionally, structures cut into the rock on the summit were probably monastic cells.

The original Church of St. Michael is thought to have been destroyed on September 11, 1275, by a major earthquake whose tremors were felt from Canterbury to Wales. It was rebuilt in the following century using local sandstone and foundation blocks from the previous structure, but it fell into ruin after the English Reformation when King Henry VIII ordered the Dissolution of the Monasteries.

Prior to its dissolution, St. Michael's Monastery had been a place of pilgrimage for medieval Catholics. Pilgrims made the steep climb up Glastonbury Tor with hard peas in their shoes as penance.

In the modern era, pilgrimages have resumed. Every summer, the Bishop of Clifton leads singing Roman Catholic pilgrims from Glastonbury Tor down to the ancient ruins at Glastonbury Abbey, where they celebrate Mass.

September evenings in Britain stay light long into the night, but the bus back to Glastonbury doesn't run that late, so I couldn't stay on the tor longer. I made my way back down and caught the bus back to town.

Calm and serene, the Daisy Centre was a respite from Glastonbury's touristy vibe and very nice to go home to, but I was hungry. Although

Daisy provided breakfast, guests were on their own for dinner. I found Rainbows End Cafe, a vegetarian restaurant on High Street with food so delicious I ate there on both nights of my stay in Glastonbury.

Figure 2-6 Inside the Rainbows End Cafe.

Chapter 3
Ley Lines and Glastonbury-ness

Waking at Daisy Centre the morning after I explored the tor was a tranquil experience. I meditated and then made my way to the kitchen, where I met Carolyn, who had just come from Sweden to work for Daisy. In addition to preparing breakfast, her duties included teaching, and leading sessions at the Centre. She also made decent coffee, which I've already said, is hard to find in Britain. Because Daisy Centre focused on spiritual matters, it was not your typical English bed-and-breakfast. But Daisy did serve a very good English breakfast.

The Daisy Centre's programs were primarily about angels, with titles such as Angelic Healing Retreat, Angels of Awakening Academy, and Angelic Healing Treatments and Therapies Weekends. Daisy also offered week-long retreats. Statues of angels dotted the grounds and stood around a koi pond. That is not to say that a plethora of other New Age ideas were unwelcome. Crystals, vortexes, and lines of energy were all up for discussion.

As I mentioned before, Glastonbury abounds with metaphysical mysteries. Legends concerning its history and sacred significance have circulated since the Middle Ages, many of those centering on King Arthur. These days, Glastonbury is said to be a major center of energy and the home of a goddess.

Daisy and I were joined for breakfast by five women who had come from London for a weekend retreat. I got a sense that Daisy's retreats

Chapter 3 Ley Lines and Glastonbury-ness

Figure 3-1 Angel statue next to a pond at Daisy Centre.

drew primarily female clients. Being surrounded by feminine energy at breakfast was a delicious experience, but the conversation quickly moved beyond my ken, drifting far afield of King Arthur.

The women discussed energy forces along ley lines, a concept with which I was not familiar. But the London women were all about it, and Daisy appeared knowledgeable on the subject. They quizzed me about whether I knew where the ley lines ran in America. I didn't have a clue.

The women taught me that ley lines are hypothetical lines of energy connecting geographical places, such as ancient sacred sites and megaliths. Ley lines and their intersection points are believed to resonate a special, mystical, or cosmic power similar to the way high-voltage electrical lines emit a measurable electromagnetic field.

The term "ley line" was coined in 1921 by amateur British archaeologist Alfred Watkins. While driving to investigate the site of an ancient Roman encampment, he stopped to get his bearings and noticed a series of straight alignments between ancient churches, standing stones, Neolithic megaliths, and geological features such as the ridgetops of the Malvern Hills in the distance. Later, he told his son, the revelation was "like a chain of fairy lights" connecting key points. He sought higher ground for a wider perspective and noticed in the scene below him that footpaths dating from ancient times followed straight trackways of line-of-sight navigation between these points.

Figure 3-2 The Malvern Hills, said by Alfred Watkins to have a ley line passing along their ridge. Photo: Daderot.‡

He presented his findings in a paper in which he quoted G. H. Piper, who in 1882 wrote, "A line drawn from the Skirrid-fawr mountain northwards to Arthur's Stone would pass over the camp and southernmost point of Hatterall Hill, Oldcastle, Longtown Castle, Urishay, and Snodhill castles." But it was Watkins who gave a name to the lines. He also theorized that the straight ancient trackways following those lines had persisted in Britain's landscape since Neolithic times.

Correct or not, Watkins was purely concerned with the archaeological implications. The association of ley lines with spiritual and mystical alignments came in the late 1960s via a book by John Michell that drew

Chapter 3 Ley Lines and Glastonbury-ness

on the concept of feng shui, a Chinese system purporting that subtle energies can be directed, reflected, or misaligned by the arrangement of natural and geometric elements. In a subsequent book, Michell theorized that Britain's ley lines met at a point equidistant from Glastonbury, Stonehenge, Goring-on-Thames and Llantwit Major. The point was at the center of a circular alignment he called the Circle of Perpetual Choirs. Michell's book also spawned a magazine, *The Ley Hunter*, which has sent believers like the women at my breakfast table searching Britain for ley lines ever since.

The longest ley line in Great Britain is called St. Michael's Ley Line. It stretches westward from the easternmost coast near Great Yarmouth on the North Sea, terminating in Penzance on the Atlantic coast. Its astronomical connection is that every May, during the Festival of St. Michael, the sun's path exactly follows the ley line, passing over Avebury and Glastonbury. How convenient for tourism. And let's not forget the name of the church at the top of Glastonbury Tor—St. Michael's.

Was there anything to this? I didn't know. I was there to trace Arthur's footsteps, after all. However, the area around Glastonbury is replete with Neolithic monuments, big and small. In America, we are most familiar with Stonehenge, but touring Britain, you soon discover that these ancient monuments, called henges, are prevalent throughout England and Wales. I visited several of them later in my trip.

Another type of Neolithic structure related to henges are cursuses—massive parallel man-made banks and ditches ranging in length from fifty meters to several kilometers. They were constructed between 3400 and 3000 BCE, and Watkins included them—along with henges—as reliable indicators of ley lines. Although I'd never heard of cursuses prior to my trip, I would later see the largest on my drive to Marlborough.

The iconic Stonehenge monument extends beyond the massive standing stones with which Americans are familiar. It is surrounded by a great circular enclosure of concentric rings formed by a ditch that's 360-feet in diameter. This outer circle is connected to the standing stones at the center by spoke-like processional pathways that run straight as a ley line. The Stonehenge layout was similar to Michell's Circle of Perpetual

Choirs, and who was I to say that wasn't the result of radiant ley lines? Hey, before breakfast, I hadn't even known what ley lines were.

After the women left the breakfast table to search for ley lines, Daisy and I continued to converse. She explained that the Daisy Centre was not named for her, but for the daisy flower which she said represented the Flower of Life with its twelve petals.

Figure 3-3 Flower of Life.

What is the Flower of Life? It is a geometrical shape composed of seven or more evenly spaced, overlapping circles of the same diameter. The space defined by the overlap of any two circles resembles a flower petal. The center of overlapping circles looks like a six-petaled flower.

I realized I'd seen this design many times before. It appears frequently in Art Nouveau, and in the work of Leonardo da Vinci, who, centuries earlier, studied the Flower of Life's form and its mathematical properties. He drew the Flower of Life itself, and incorporated some of its components in several of his works.

The earliest images of the Flower of Life are found in the 6,000-year-old Temple of Osiris at Abydos, Egypt. Other examples can be found in Phoenician, Assyrian, Indian, Asian, Middle Eastern, and medieval art.

The Flower of Life contains within it what Plato called sacred geometry. By drawing straight lines between the centers of the circles that make up the Flower of Life, one can delineate all five Platonic solids—geometric figures that Plato said were the basis of all structures. Other

CHAPTER 3 LEY LINES AND GLASTONBURY-NESS

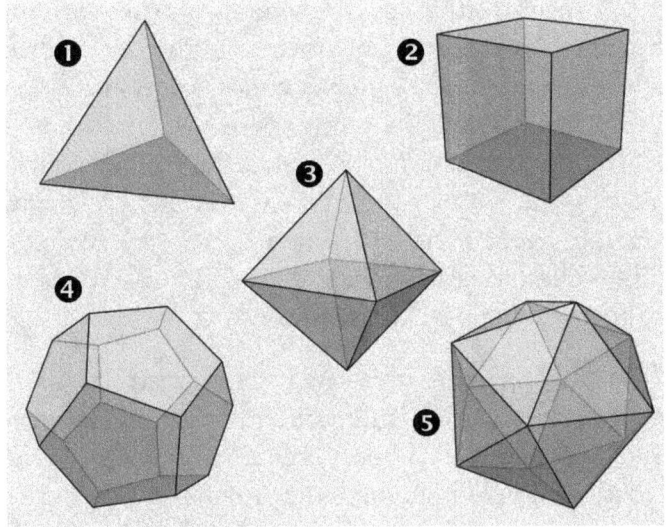

Figure 3-4 Platonic Solids:
1. Tetrahedron
2. Hexahedron,
3. Octahedron
4. Dodecahedron
5. Icosahedron

mystical shapes found within the Flower of Life, include the Kabbalah's Tree of Life and the Egyptian Eye of Horus.

Daisy had my head spinning by the time I left the breakfast table.

Glastonbury is the most charming of cities, a must-see in England, and exactly the heart of the Arthurian legend I had come here to trace. It is, though, open to every unorthodox philosophy anyone wants to pursue and has been that way for two thousand years or more.

I came to Glastonbury with the primary intention of touring its abbey, but that was within walking distance of Daisy Centre, and I decided it could wait. I also wanted to visit South Cadbury, the site that had once been Camelot. I started the car and motored south, following route A39 to B3151. After circling several roundabouts, I made my way onto the A303. Along the way, I thought of a few more examples of Glastonbury's eclectic beliefs.

A myth of more recent origin is that of the Glastonbury Zodiac. According to this myth, an astrological zodiac of immense dimensions had been carved into the land along the ancient hedgerows and trackways Watkins studied in 1921. And prominently featured as an astrological sign in the Glastonbury Zodiac is—what else?—the Glastonbury Tor.

25

This came about in 1927, when Katharine Maltwood, an artist with an interest in the occult, came up with the theory that a gigantic zodiac eleven miles in diameter existed in the Somerset countryside surrounding Glastonbury. To prove her point, she commissioned aerial photographs of the region. In them, she saw the twelve traditional zodiac symbols subtly outlined by the rivers, contours, and ancient trackways of the Somerset landscape. Some were delineated by natural geological features in the land, while other signs were defined by the edges of man-made things like roadways and field boundaries.

Maltwood proposed that this ancient zodiac had been constructed approximately five thousand years earlier. The problem was that the majority of her eleven-mile zodiac circle had been underwater at that time. Not to mention that roads and field boundaries she included didn't exist back then. So, if someone sees a zodiac in the land below, it may have more in common with a Rorschach ink blot than the authentic ancient monoliths that dot the English countryside elsewhere.

Maltwood died in 1961, but her Glastonbury Zodiac lives on. In 2009, three enterprising astrologers moved to Glastonbury and began offering Zodiac Mystery School workshops and tours.

It's not just the pagans and the occult that have a claim on Glastonbury. Christianity in Britain dates back to 63 CE when Romans occupied Britain. Joseph of Arimathea was a merchant who bought and shipped tin from southwest Britain, where it had been mined since the Phoenician era. If his name rings a bell, it is because Joseph was the rich man who gave his tomb for Jesus to be buried in.

Some years after Christ's crucifixion, Joseph left Jerusalem to settle in Britain and founded Britain's first Christian church. A local leader, King Arviragus, gave him 12 hides of land (about 120 acres) on which to build his church. Five centuries later, the site became home to Glastonbury Abbey, which I still had every intention of visiting.

Then there is the Chalice Well, a natural spring in the valley between Glastonbury Tor and Chalice Hill. Actually, there are two springs within a hundred meters of each other. The White Spring discharges

CHAPTER 3 LEY LINES AND GLASTONBURY-NESS

almost 95,000 liters of water per day. Its high concentrations of calcium carbonate leave white calcite deposits, hence the name. The nearby Red Spring contains dissolved ferrous oxide that leaves reddish deposits.

Figure 3-5 Chalice Well with a cover designed by Frederick Bligh Bond. Photo: Kurt Thomas Hunt.‡

Both springs provided local people with a practical source of clean water for millennia. But in October 1750, the Chancellor of North Wootton, afflicted with asthma and coughing spells, claimed that he had been healed by waters from the Red Spring. Soon after, the spring became known as Chalice Well, and experienced a surge in visitors. A 1751 magazine reported that ten thousand people had come to Glastonbury to drink from the well. Local entrepreneurs took advantage of the publicity and began bottling and shipping the water to apothecaries for resale.

A myth says the spring's red color is from the rust of nails used in Christ's crucifixion, which Joseph of Arimathea deposited in the well. Not to be outdone, goddess worshipers claimed the spring symbolized the menstrual flow of the Celtic goddess Brigid, who guards sacred springs. Supposedly, one gains poetic wisdom, metalsmithing skills, and healing abilities by drinking from her well. Ceremonial celebrations at the Chalice Well include an annual procession carrying an effigy of the goddess up the tor. (I presume this happens on a different date than the Roman Catholic pilgrimages from the tor to the abbey.)

In 1919, a well covering designed by church architect Frederick Bligh Bond was donated to the site. Today, a trust runs the Chalice Well for "spiritual-inspirational" uses and offers a quiet garden in which to sit and meditate after drinking the waters. And of course, there's a gift shop, too.

In recent years, there have been reports of mysterious light phenomena at Glastonbury Tor. In 1981, people climbing the hill saw a strange writhing light arc from St. Michael's Tower to the ground near Chalice Well. Author Paul Devereux, editor of *The Ley Hunter* magazine, also reported witnessing strange lights in 1991.

I was still thinking about all of this as I turned off route A303 and arrived in South Cadbury. Signs directed visitors to the site of Camelot and the associated car park. When I turned into the drive, I saw an ominous billboard warning tourists to lock their cars and remove all valuables as the area was plagued with car thieves. Fortunately, I'd left

Chapter 3 Ley Lines and Glastonbury-ness

everything but my camera back at Daisy Centre. I slipped it into my pocket and locked the car.

Too bad Arthur's brave company of knights wasn't around to defend Camelot's car park.

Chapter 4
Camelot

Mine was the lone car in the South Cadbury parking lot on an autumn weekday, and I was the sole tourist present—a dubious situation in light of the sign warning about thieves. The car park also contained a large placard detailing the history of the Cadbury site as a fortress and stronghold, with illustrations of what it was believed to have looked like in King Arthur's day.

I walked out to the narrow paved road I'd arrived on and looked for traffic in both directions. There wasn't any. To my right stretched South

Figure 4-1 Sign with drawing of Castle excavation based on the work of Leslie Alcock in 1966.

Cadbury such as it was. The village consisted of three or four blocks of buildings strung out along Chapel Road. I could see a pub and a church. But if you were imagining I smelled the fragrance of delicious chocolate, you'd be wrong. Famous Cadbury chocolate comes from Birmingham, England—about 140 miles away. The company was named for two brothers who founded it, not the village in which I stood.

I crossed the narrow paved road to a sign at the entrance of a gravel lane: "Castle Lane leading to Camelot Fort." A sign beneath it pointed me in the right direction: "Pedestrian Walkway to Cadbury Castle." Although the UK Ancient Monuments Act protects Cadbury Castle, it is situated on private land. The lane passed between two buildings that looked to be made of ancient stonework, but were fitted with modern windows. The buildings would be considered old by United States standards, but Brits think anything less than eight hundred years old is relatively new.

Figure 4-2 Lane leading to the castle site.

Figure 4-3 Rolling path is the top of buried castle walls.

A hundred feet past the buildings, the lane turned from a gravel drive into a tree-lined dirt path wide enough for a tractor. It rose at an incline, and as I hiked up the hill, the banks on either side of the path became higher. Soon I found myself following an ancient trackway depression three or four feet below the level of the surrounding land.

After about a quarter of a mile, I crested the hill and came out of the woods into a pasture. The perimeter of the plateau consisted of soft hill shapes that, according to the placard in the parking lot, covered buried walls. In what might have once been the castle courtyard, cows looked at me without fear as they wandered around grazing.

The word "castle" conjures the image of a medieval fortress with towers and battlements, gleaming white stone walls, and fancy turrets flying the banner of the latest knight to win a fair damsel. But no, Cadbury Castle had actually been a hill-fort, and certainly never resembled the Camelot we see in movies. King Arthur lived from the late fifth century to the mid-sixth century—a good six hundred years before stonemasons began building castles in Britain. The fortified hill itself was the castle, and it was constructed mostly of wood, with earthen embankments, built upon an isolated mount of limestone and sandstone. Still, it was no small thing. It enclosed eighteen acres with walls ranging from fourteen to sixteen feet thick. Its summit is about five hundred feet above sea level and offers a wide view of the central Somerset countryside.

I walked the three-quarter mile perimeter, which rose and fell like a child's rollercoaster. Beneath my feet, scientific proof of the castle's existence had been discovered in the Victorian era when the Rector of South Cadbury, Reverend James Bennett, carried out the first small excavation. In a paper published in 1890, he describes cutting a trench through the top rampart, the very path I was walking. He correctly surmised that the castle was built up in layers over a long time.

Next, he went to the plateau and dug down to a pit in the bedrock. There he discovered pottery scraps, and a primitive hand mill used to grind grain. The bottom of the pit contained a large, flat stone. One of Bennett's assistants thought it covered the opening of a cave. But upon lifting it, they found only another large, flat stone.

Dwellings within the ramparts were built of wood, thatch, and wattle. Wattle is made by weaving pliable, finger-width branches into crosshatch lattices. (See Figure 4-4) The wattle can then be attached to a wooden frame and plastered with mud to form walls, similar to the way modern stucco houses are made by plastering laths. Wattle without mud was sometimes used in a way similar to modern chicken wire fence, as a pen for fowl and small livestock, or to keep wild animals out of gardens. I'd written about wattle in *Lancelot's Grail*, but until my walk up the hill to Camelot, I'd never seen it. I photographed it to study further when I returned home.

In 1913, British archeologist H. St. George Gray excavated near the hill-fort's southwest entrance. He found objects that dated to the late Iron Age, before the Roman conquest. It is now understood that the site was at times a military stronghold and a center of trade and culture from 3,000 BCE through the early eleventh century CE.

Figure 4-4 Example of wattle (made from woven branches).

Beginning as a modest Bronze Age settlement, it grew during the Iron Age into a large, spectacular hill-fort town, and was the capital of Dorset and the southern Somerset territories of the Durotriges, a confederacy of Celtic tribes that lived in Britain before the Roman invasion, which began in 43 CE.

The Romans initially left Cadbury alone, but they cleared out the town in 70 CE, relocating those they didn't kill to other settlements. Toward the end of the Roman period, people returned to the hill-fort; and in about 500 CE, they undertook a massive refortification. Timber and stone replaced the earlier earthen banks. Posts for a new southwest gate were embedded in solid rock. In the center of the defenses stood an immense hall constructed of wood. The scale of the work implies that there was a highly organized, wealthy, and advanced military society behind it.

The only surviving written record from the fifth century reveals that Britain divided into small kingdoms. Oral traditions say these kingdoms

CHAPTER 4 CAMELOT

engaged in a series of battles under the leadership of a man called Arthur, to fend off the invading Saxons. The fort atop the place where I stood was strategically situated to defend southwest Britain and could easily have been the base from which Arthur led his knights to final victory at the Battle of Badon.

Figure 4-5 A stone marker atop Cadbury Castle site with stainless steel plaque showing the distance to various sites that could exchange signals with the hillfort.

I paused my circumnavigation of the fort's perimeter when I reached a modern stone marker. It was a round pillar capped by a stainless steel plate etched with arrows pointing toward various ancient sites and giving their distance in miles. I was amazed that I could see the Glastonbury Tor, which the plaque said was thirty-seven miles away. I read that archeology students had conducted an experiment in which they lit a signal fire here and were able to see it from Glastonbury Tor. This makes a very good case for the ability of ancient commanders to signal each other in case of attack or other important incident.

After Gray's 1913 investigation of the site, further archeological efforts were stymied by two world wars. Then, when a portion of the field was plowed in the mid-1950s, local archeologist, Mary Hartfield, picked up flints and potsherds from the upturned soil. Dr. Ralegh Radford identified them as being similar to the type of imported pottery he'd found at Tintagel, a site on the Cornish coast that dated back to the days of Arthur. This proved that someone who possessed enough wealth to import luxury goods had lived at the Cadbury site about the time of Arthur. This wasn't news to the locals, who for fourteen hundred years had been saying that Cadbury was the site of Camelot.

However, it wasn't until 1542 that King Henry VIII's chief antiquarian, John Leland, cemented the idea by putting it in writing: "At the very south end of the church of South-Cadbyri standeth Camallate, sometime a famous town or castle, upon a very tor or hill, wonderfully enstrengthened of nature.... The people can tell nothing there but that they have heard say Arthur much resorted to Camalat."

Dr. Radford's confirmation of Hartfield's findings led to the formation of the Camelot Research Committee. This committee carried out large-scale excavations of the site from 1966 to 1970 under the direction of Leslie Alcock, professor of archeology at the University of Glasgow, and one of the leading archeologists studying Early Medieval Britain.

Copious findings at the site proved that Iron Age occupants had not only built the earthwork defenses but also reconstructed the top bank several times. A community flourished on the plateau for centuries prior to the Roman occupation. Evidence uncovered in the dig showed that the occupants of Cadbury Castle were not relocated until decades after the Romans claimed this part of Britain.

For the remainder of the Roman period, the hill-fort stayed empty. Then, after the Romans withdrew from Britain, Saxons began to push in. Across Britain, fifth-century Britons refurbished and strengthened the ancient hill-forts for housing as well as protection.

When Professor Alcock's excavation team reached the layers pertaining to Arthur's time, the archeological finds far exceeded anyone's prediction. In a commanding position, centered on the highest part of the hill, they discovered the foundation of Arthur's Palace—a timber hall sixty-three feet long by thirty-four feet wide. Post-holes cut in the bedrock identified where the walls had stood. Inside, trenches marked where partitions had divided large and small rooms. Its outline resembled the hall at Castle Dore, another Iron Age fort that Radford had investigated. But the Cadbury site suggested more skillful workmanship. Had the Knights of the Round Table assembled, feasted, listened to minstrels, and planned campaigns in this building?

Workers also uncovered smaller buildings near the main hall. One may have been the kitchen, and others part of an Arthurian complex. At the castle's southwest entry, the archeologists found the remains of a sophisticated gatehouse from the same period. A ten-foot-wide cobbled road passed through double doors into a nearly square wooden tower, then out and into the castle grounds through similar doors on the opposite side.

Additionally, Alcock's team had dug into the perimeter embankment on which I stood. They cut cross-sections in several places, revealing strata showing that the ramparts had been rebuilt numerous times in the centuries preceding Arthur. But during his period, the refurbishments became grand. At the strata that represented the Arthurian Age, they found a dry stone wall that was sixteen feet thick. Gaps in the wall, marked by rotted ancient timber showed where massive posts had once supported breastworks on the outside to protect men standing on the wall. Beams ran crosswise to bind the structures together, supporting a platform, and perhaps wooden watch towers.

The timber bracing and the superstructure of the wall itself were similar to other hill-forts the British Celts built before the Roman conquest. But reconstruction performed in the Arthurian period incorporated fragments of masonry salvaged from abandoned Roman ruins.

When the project concluded in 1970, only a fraction of the site had been opened, but the discoveries had been plentiful. The archeologists dutifully refilled their excavations, reburying all that had once been Camelot. But was it really? None of the artifacts had Arthur's name on them. No sign on the gatehouse said, "Welcome to ye old Camallate." That would have been too much to hope for.

So, were Cadbury Castle and Camelot one and the same? The case is circumstantial, but the probability is strong. After five years of research, the evidence showed that the site had been reoccupied and refortified on a colossal scale during the Arthurian time period by a leader with uncommon resources. In the center of the castle, this leader had constructed what, for Arthur's time, was a large building along with numerous smaller ones. The encampment surrounding the fort could hold a thousand men, plus ancillary staff, followers, and families. If this leader wasn't King Arthur, he was an Arthur-like figure.

It's likely that Cadbury is Camelot not only because this hill-fort was converted into a vast citadel during the right time period, but also because no other known post-Roman sites in Britain are candidates. Although numerous other hill-forts were reoccupied after the Romans departed, the areas within their ramparts were much smaller, and none served as a base for sizable combat forces. While a few of the other sites showed where walls had been rebuilt, no other place exhibited new fortifications even close to the elaborate gatehouse and stone-and-timber ramparts of Cadbury/Camelot.

As I stood on one of the reburied rampart walls, I recalled an old friend who said he could look out on a historic site like Gettysburg and see events as they unfolded. I thought of him that day up on the castle hill-fort and wished he were with me to describe what he could see.

Below the hill, to the left of the path up to the hill-fort is a well called Arthur's Well. An old track running towards Glastonbury is named Arthur's Lane. As early as 1586, the highest part of the hill was on record as Arthur's Palace, even though the building's buried remains wouldn't be unearthed for another four centuries. Perhaps the locals had been right when, in 1542, they told John Leland this site was Camelot.

Departing the hill-fort, I returned to the main road. Looking to my left, I saw the one place I could visit in South Cadbury that would allow me to say with certainty I'd been in Camelot—the local pub, aptly named

Chapter 4 Camelot

Camelot Inn.

I stopped there for a glass of cold cider. The pub's backyard had a lovely green lawn and tables with umbrellas. Rivulets of sweat ran down the outside of my glass as I made notes in my journal. What a pleasant way to end my field trip to Camelot.

Figure 4-6 The Camelot pub.

Figure 5-1 Arches at left were the original entrance to the Glastonbury Abbey grounds.

Chapter 5
Glastonbury Abbey

The principal attraction in the town of Glastonbury is the ancient abbey ruins. I'd saved it for last. Now I intended to explore it fully. I made the short walk from Daisy Centre and entered via a paved walkway that, although wide enough for a lorry, was restricted to pedestrian traffic. On my left was a tan stone wall at least seven hundred years old. Perpendicular to the wall were several arched portals that may have once held gates. These portals were blocked by large flower pots that prevented visitors from walking through them.

The walkway ended two or three hundred feet from the street where I'd entered. A gift shop on my left had once been the abbey gatehouse. I turned right and entered the abbey grounds, thirty-six acres of park land. In the distance stood the ruined church's stone walls, and further on, a large building with a cone-shaped roof. I could also see a large manor house beyond the park. The previous owners had lived there before the property was acquired by the National Trust.

Two days before the equinox, the official start of autumn, the grass was still lush green, the September air crisp, and the sun bright. An almost palpable sense of this place washed over me. I intuited history I didn't yet know, and knowledge I needed for my novel awaited.

Figure 5-2 A remaining wall fragment of the destroyed cathedral.

Chapter 5 Glastonbury Abbey

My eye was drawn to tall structural stone fragments standing in the distance, and my feet followed. In its day, the church was huge. The nave had been 220-feet long and 45-feet wide, the choir 155-feet in length, and the transept 160-feet long. In addition to the main sanctuary area, there had been two chapels within the structure, St Joseph's and the Lady Chapel. Each exceeded 100-feet in length.

The walls of the Lady Chapel, which is below ground level, still survive. (See Figure 5-4). When I entered, I looked up. The church floor should have been overhead, and the church roof above that. Both were missing so I saw open sky. I estimated the surrounding walls to be fifty or sixty feet high. A drawing illustrating the abbey complex at the time of its dissolution showed the great church to be two or three times the height of the Lady Chapel. That would mean the church walls were 150 to 180 feet tall.

Figure 5-3 Surviving portion of the cathedral.

Figure 5-4 The subterranean Lady Chapel was once covered by the now-missing church floor.

This wasn't the first abbey at Glastonbury, but thanks to King Henry VIII dissolving the abbeys during his reign, it was the last. What remains of the structure are a dozen separate sections of the outer walls, portions of the clerestory and triforium arcades that supported the central square tower. Among the surviving stonework are the outer walls of the chancel aisles and retroquire behind the high altar. The south nave aisle wall, west front, and a chapel or porch at the west end also survive.

The original abbey was built on the site of the first Christian church in Britain, which was founded by Joseph of Arimathea and eleven other early Christians. They built a church of wattles and dab, and lived out their lives in austerity and prayer.

The Holy Thorn Tree at the abbey—subject of mystery, myth, and fact—is a possible descendant from the days of that first church. The large tree

Chapter 5 Glastonbury Abbey

had wild, ragged-looking branches that spanned at least twenty feet, and it stood as tall as a nearby building. I walked over to read a placard that identified it. It's a mystery because the tree is a variety of hawthorn that grows in the Mideast and is not found elsewhere in Britain. The myth is that after Joseph of Arimathea thrust his staff into the ground in that spot, the Holy Thorn Tree took root and flourished. The tree before me was purported to be grown from a cutting of the original tree. It flowers in late spring and again around Christmastime, whereas the hawthorn variety native to Britain only flowers once a year.

That first abbey at Glastonbury was constructed of wood during the Dark Ages after the Romans left. The earliest written mention of it occurs in a biography about St. Patrick who lived from 387 to 460 CE. According to the account, St. Patrick returned from Ireland and became a leader of a group of hermits at Glastonbury. One day he climbed through dense woods and discovered a ruined, ancient oratory. Some believed it to have been built by Joseph of Arimathea. If so, it would have been rebuilt several times, as it is unlikely the original wattle and mud would have survived into St. Patrick's era.

Some historians initially questioned the notion that Glastonbury Abbey had existed that early. Then archeological excavations unearthed Romano-British pottery at the west end of the cloister dating to before the Dark Ages. Ceramic wine jars imported from the Mediterranean were also found in strata lower than the present foundations.

In 712, five decades after the Saxons defeated the Britons, the abbey was reconstructed of stone at the direction of Saxon King Ine of Wessex. Then, in the tenth century, the church was enlarged and cloisters were added. Monks dug a canal linking the abbey to the River Brue, allowing them to transport stone from the abbey's quarries to the Glastonbury site. Later, this water transportation system was used to bring produce, grain, wine, and fish from the abbey's outlying properties. As the eleventh century dawned, new canals and channels were added, making Glastonbury Abbey the center of a large water transport network.

Glastonbury's wealth made it a plum prize in the Norman Conquest (1066) and Norman abbots took over. Skilled Norman stonemasons further enlarged the church and added other magnificent buildings. Then, in 1184, a fire destroyed much of what the Norman abbots had built.

In 1191, while rebuilding the burned abbey, monks uncovered an ancient grave on the south side of the Lady Chapel. It contained two skeletons, a male and a female. Beneath a covering stone, they found a leaden cross with the Latin inscription "Hic jacet sepultus inclitus rex Arthurus in insula Avalonia." Translation: "Here lies interred the famous King Arthur on the Isle of Avalon." The female was presumed to be Queen Guinevere, whom legend claimed had been buried next to her husband.

I walked over to a grave plot, which was outlined by an eight-inch-high stone border. (Figure 5-5). A placard stated that in 1278 Arthur and Guinevere's remains were relocated from the original grave to a black marble tomb at this spot in the presence of King Edward I and Queen Eleanor. The tomb survived until the abbey's dissolution.

In hindsight, many today question whether the skeletons were really those of Arthur and Guinevere or merely wishful thinking on the part of the monks—wishful thinking that was then propagated to enhance the abbey's coffers. Since King Henry VIII destroyed the tomb along with the rest of the abbey in 1539, we'll never know. Certainly King Edward I believed the skeleton to be Arthur. Two historians of Edward's period documented the grave site, Giraldus Cambrensis in 1193, and Roger of Coggeshall in 1216.

I found interesting that both historians said the grave was located between two pyramids. The pyramids were also confirmed in the writings of William of Malmesbury a few years later. However, I saw no sign of pyramids nor any mention of them at the site. But I wondered what the heck pyramids were doing on the grounds of a twelfth-century monastery. Moreover, why hadn't all the hippies in Glastonbury made a thing of it? I could envision a New Age shop on High Street selling miniature pyramids.

Chapter 5 Glastonbury Abbey

Figure 5-5 Stone border outlining the site of King Arthur's Tomb where monks discovered the grave of King Arthur and a female presumed to have been Queen Guinevere.

Whatever the case with the skeletons' authenticity, the reconstruction of Glastonbury Abbey was completed after their discovery. By the Middle Ages, it was the country's second largest religious institution. Only Westminster Abbey in London was bigger. Enormously wealthy, the abbey's estates stretched from the southern coast of England all the way to the Welsh border. Tithe barns were built to hold the crops paid to the abbey.

Consecutive abbots of Glastonbury were powerful and prestigious men who lived in splendor. The Abbot's Hall stood eighty feet tall. Privileged pilgrims, nobility, and even kings and queens, filled the abbey coffers with money and stayed in special apartments at the south end of the Abbot's Hall. The building is gone now. Only a partial wall remains to tell us where it stood.

Attached to the former Hall was the Abbot's Kitchen, the only building on the entire property that survived intact and has been restored. The Abbot's Kitchen was an octagon-shaped structure with a tall, conical roof. An opening at the top created a draft that kept three fireplaces roaring. There, cooks prepared sumptuous meals to serve the abbot's guests—evidence of the abbey's abundance and dominion.

A special apartment was added to the south end of the Abbot's Hall for King Henry VII's visit. Henry VII, the first Tudor king, assumed the throne at the end of the War of Roses, a civil war between two rival families. During the war, things in England had become so unsettled that a wall was constructed around the abbey precincts. Henry VII resolved lingering disharmony by marrying the eldest daughter of the rival York faction.

Figure 5-6 A drawing showing Glastonbury Abbey as it was in 1539.

CHAPTER 5 GLASTONBURY ABBEY

In 1493, Pilgrims' Inn was built across the road from the abbey entrance to accommodate visitors who didn't warrant a room in the Abbot's Hall. After the abbey's dissolution, the Inn was given to the Duke of

Figure 5-7 Pilgrims Inn, built in 1493, as it looked in 2009.

Somerset, who leased it to George Cowdrey. By the nineteenth century it was known as The George Hotel. It is still operational today as The George Hotel and Pilgrims' Inn, preserving both legacies. The inn is a three-story stone structure with carved panels above the entrance bearing the coats of arms for both the Abbey and King Edward IV. I'd stopped in there the day I arrived in Glastonbury, while looking to rent a room before finding Daisy Centre.

The next Tudor king, Henry VIII, is best remembered for his six marriages and for separating the Church of England from papal authority after the pope refused to grant him a divorce. He followed this with the Dissolution of Monasteries, which disbanded all abbeys, monasteries, priories, convents, and friaries in England, Wales, and Ireland. At the beginning of the Dissolution, almost 900 of these religious cloisters existed. Five years later, there were none. The crown appropriated their income, disposed of their assets, and sold off monastic lands.

In September 1539, three of the king's men arrived at Glastonbury Abbey on the orders of Thomas Cromwell. The abbey was stripped of its valuables. The abbot, Richard Whiting, who had supported Henry VIII as head of the church, was surprised and resisted. Then, on November 15, 1539, Henry had Glastonbury Abbey burned, and had the abbot, hanged, drawn, and quartered on Glastonbury Tor. Things were never the same for the abbey after that.

The abbey's contents were needlessly mishandled. For instance, the skeletons that may or may not have been Arthur and Guinevere were lost. The abbey also had an extensive library. Books that generations of monks had huddled over, transcribing and illuminating, were lost—not just religious books, but books on natural history, politics, and the law. Pages of priceless manuscripts littered the streets in the aftermath.

The abbey buildings were stripped of lead, a valuable metal at the time, and the dressed stones were hauled away for use in other buildings. It was said that King Henry VIII sat in a room on an upper floor of the Pilgrims' Inn and watched the abbey burn. However, that part of the

Chapter 5 Glastonbury Abbey

story is false. The abbey walls were blown up by a subsequent owner, who wanted to reuse the stones.

The site of the abbey was given to the Duke of Somerset and later passed through several other hands. It remained privately owned until 1908, when it was acquired by the Bath and Wells dioceses of the Church of England. The entire site is now protected by the Ancient Monuments Act and is owned by the UK National Trust, which will surely protect it better than kings and aristocrats did.

Figure 6-1 Exterior of the Abbot's Kitchen.

Chapter 6
The Abbot's Kitchen

Still at Glastonbury abbey, I opened the heavy wooden door of the octagon-shaped building and entered the Abbot's Kitchen, the only fully restored abbey building. In this large open space with stone walls and floor, round wooden beams extended upward from the eight sides to meet at the apex, supporting a tall, conical ceiling. A gothic arch at the far end of the room had once connected the kitchen to the now missing Abbot's Hall.

Several other tourists entered behind me. A docent dressed in a simple monk's robe welcomed us and began his lecture. He pointed to an opening at the top of the ceiling where the support beams met and explained its purpose, to create a draft that kept three fireplaces roaring. These were nothing like our modern living room fireplaces. They were so large I could have stood inside one and not been able to touch the top of it. (See Figure 21-1). One held a giant, three-tier, wrought iron rack containing two fake pigs on its spits. Another contained a brick oven for baking bread.

Work tables used for food preparation held a variety of terracotta bowls, crocks, amphorae, cups, and goblets. Some had been glazed, others not. An array of faux vegetable props filled the bowls and baskets under the tables. Dried herbs hung on a large rack on one side of the room. Since this building existed long before modern plumbing, the kitchen didn't have a sink. (Figure 6-2).

Figure 6-2 Interior of the Abbot's Kitchen.

Chapter 6 The Abbot's Kitchen

The docent described not only the kitchen, but also the monks' diet, daily life at the abbey, and the abbot's guests. These were exactly the kind of details I'd come to England to learn for my novel. Of special interest to me, he said that women from the surrounding town had worked in the Abbot's Kitchen as cooks, bakers, and chefs. Younger monks had helped the women prepare banquets for the abbey's important guests. "Nothing went on, mind you," the docent said. "Monks took their chastity vows seriously, but the ladies provided a change of scenery."

This was perfect. My novel was about a brother and sister who were abandoned at an abbey as children, and grew up working for the abbot. The sister, Alura, worked in the kitchen as one of the kitchen ladies. Now I'd found a historical basis for this plot point. Although the building I was standing in had been restored to the way it appeared in the fourteenth century and my novel was set in the sixth century, it would do.

The docent described the abbots as powerful and prestigious men who understood the importance of kowtowing to all the important nobility who came to the abbey. On a typical day, the Abbot's Kitchen was a hive of activity as the kitchen staff prepared magnificent banquets and sumptuous feasts for the abbot's privileged guests.

Situated at the hub of southwest Britain's network of canals and river channels, the abbey imported good Bordeaux wine through the ports of Bridgewater and Bristol. Grains, meats, fruits, cheeses, and produce flowed into the abbey kitchens from its estates, which extended for fifty miles. The monks also raised vegetables on the abbey grounds and kept an extensive herb garden.

The abbey had two kitchens: the Abbot's Kitchen, which prepared meat dishes and delicacies for the abbot's guests, and a smaller, separate kitchen of similar architectural design where vegetarian dishes were prepared for the monks. They ate one large meal a day consisting of soup, cheese, plenty of fruits or vegetables, and one pound of bread. Along with that, they had two cooked dishes, typically beans or eggs. Once the Saxons introduced ale to Britain, the monks also received ale with their meal; before that, they probably drank cider.

Figure 6-3 Costumed docent explaining abbey life to a tour group.

The docent remarked that monks who assisted the ladies in the Abbot's Kitchen would sample the meat now and then. I worked this tidbit into *Lancelot's Grail* by having Alura's brother, Frith, frequently visit the

Chapter 6 The Abbot's Kitchen

Abbot's Kitchen to snatch slices of meat off the carving table. Frith also sampled the imported wine, ostensibly to make sure the abbot wasn't poisoned. It must have been challenging for monks who lived a much more frugal existence than the abbot to dine in the monks' kitchen on a plainer diet after working around the aroma of rich foods and roasting meat.

Still in the Abbot's Kitchen, the docent told our tour group about other buildings that no longer existed. He also described other aspects of abbey life. Later, I would incorporate this information into my novel to lend it historical authenticity.

Glastonbury Abbey's extensive library had been situated in the cloister's north walk and had carrels in which monks wrote and studied. Books were enclosed in wooden cupboards when not in use.

In the abbey scriptorium monks transcribed and illuminated the manuscripts that filled the library. Their work was done by hand. They dipped quills in ink and wrote on parchment. The five outer wing feathers of the goose or swan were considered the best for use as quills. The monks would have to regularly re-cut the writing point (nib) as it became worn through use. This, of course, shortened the life of the quill. Those who illuminated the manuscripts with colored images needed multiple quills, one for each color of ink.

Before a monk could work in the scriptorium he had to know how to read and write Latin. A method of teaching Latin to the youngest monks was to have the boys arrange pebbles in their shoes in the shape of an alphabet character and then wear the shoes all day. The impressions the stones made on their soles would fix the shape of the letter in their minds.

The docent explained that it wasn't easy to gain entry to the order. A routine test of the aspirant's stamina and sincerity was to make a boy stand outside and knock on the door for four days before admitting him.

Glastonbury Abbey lay along the old Roman road. In the Dark Ages, there were few points along the road where travelers could stay, and they were far apart. The Christian monastery offered a safe refuge to travelers seeking a night's sleep and a meal. As the abbey's importance increased, the pilgrim traffic resulted in the growth of a surrounding village with a blacksmith, a livery service, groomsmen, hay, and feed-grain. Travelers and surrounding farmers could buy necessary supplies at the village marketplace. But the aforementioned Pilgrim's Inn wouldn't be built until centuries later.

After the docent finished his presentation, I wandered the grounds, and imagined where the monks hoed the gardens. I studied a drawing that showed the size of the church and the location of various buildings (Figure 5-6). I fixed in my mind the paths my characters would take from the kitchen to the abbey gate, between the church and the abbot's quarters, and from the monk's kitchen to the refectory. I stayed until closing time, mentally revising and adding scenes to the manuscript I had waiting at home.

In the novel, I chose not to make Glastonbury the abbey where my characters lived. It was too large and important for my fictional setting. But in many respects, my imagined abbey incorporated all that I'd seen at Glastonbury. My editor suggested the name Abbey of St. Benignus. That worked on several levels. First, there wasn't an actual abbey with that name. Second, St. Benignus was baptized by St. Patrick and became his favorite disciple. Benignus accompanied his master on his travels, assisting in his missionary work. Since St. Patrick had resided in Glastonbury, it was plausible that Benignus could have founded an abbey somewhere in the surrounding countryside.

Chapter 7
A Surprising Meditation

When Glastonbury Abbey closed for the night, it was suppertime. Satisfied with what I'd learned that day, I returned to the vegetarian restaurant where I'd eaten the previous night. While my food was prepared, I dictated some notes—a solitary diner talking to a small black recorder in his fist. No one paid any mind.

After a satisfying meal, I returned to the Daisy Centre. Daisy told me the main room where they held programs was available now. If I wanted to meditate there, I was welcome to use it. The large room was illuminated by candlelight and had a sufficient number of comfortable chairs for her workshop participants.

Figure 7-1 Meditation room inside Daisy Centre.

I thanked her, entered the room, and sat on a chair with a thick cushion. I brought my legs up, tucking one under and folding the other across my lap in a yogic posture called half-lotus. I closed my eyes and began my evening meditation practice.

I have a confession. I've made light of Glastonbury's New Age shops and the community's obsession with esoteric matters. In fact, I, too, follow spiritual teachings that may seem unorthodox to others. Daily, I meditate using Kriya Yoga, an ancient technique brought to the West from high in the Himalayas by a lineage of gurus. I am not authorized to reveal the actual methods of this form of yoga practice except in the most general terms. However, for those who are interested, instruction in Kriya Yoga is readily available from several organizations founded by gurus of the lineage.

The loose idea behind Kriya Yoga is that all living things have a current of energy, or life force that keeps them alive. The current of life energy causes breath to move. Ancient yogis discovered that controlled breathing patterns can affect the movement of this current. The yogis called this technique pranayama, or control of the life force. Kriya Yoga is an advanced form of pranayama by which the life force current is circulated up and down the spine to connect with the point where life energy enters the body. When the current connects with that point, the yogi experiences a supernormal flow of energy and a sense of ecstasy.

I do not know how long I'd been meditating before members of Daisy's weekend workshop began coming into the room for a group meditation. Daisy invited me to stay.

Once everyone in her group was seated, she began a guided meditation. I resumed my Kriya Yoga practice, but in the distance, I heard her soothing voice invoke angels and rays of lights in different colors. Let me explain. In meditation, one can be absorbed in the conscious flow of energy yet disinterestedly aware of what is happening externally. It is analogous to having a fascinating conversation with a dinner companion while a server takes an order at the next table. You peripherally hear what is said at the next table, but it isn't compelling enough to divert your attention.

Chapter 7 A Surprising Meditation

When Daisy's guided meditation ended, she brought the group back to a grounded state. Moving around the room, she discussed her perception of each person's experience. When she came to me, she said the room had been full of astral yogis who came to the meditation, presumably because my gurus had appeared during the session.

I had not witnessed the astral beings she noted, but I sometimes sense my guru in meditation, as perhaps I had that night. To give Daisy credit, her guided meditation made me feel light and uplifted, and I returned to my room feeling peaceful and happy. Daisy Centre had, indeed, been a good place to stay.

Daisy has since sold the Glastonbury Daisy Centre and it is now the Sri Gour Kripa Dham-Bhakti Yoga Ashram.

Chapter 8
Camlann and Tintagel

Before leaving Glastonbury on Monday, I ate breakfast with Daisy and Carolyn. The weekend guests had already returned to London and I would soon be departing for Tintagel, a castle and village on the Atlantic coast reputed to be King Arthur's birthplace.

Figure 8-1 Camlann battlefield, the site of King Arthur's final battle.

Chapter 8 Camlann and Tintagel

I packed the car, bid Daisy farewell, and drove for a little over two hours to the village of Camelford. Just beyond it was Camlann, the site of King Arthur's final battle. I parked and walked until I located an informational sign identifying the battlefield. I followed a stony path across the battleground, a field overgrown with thick, shin-high grass. (Figure 8-1).

In a half-dozen places, archeological digs had unearthed the remnants of ancient stone buildings. A sign sketched the location of the buildings that had previously been uncovered. It also marked current excavations and noted that future archeological digs were scheduled. The site was protected by woven wire fencing attached to sturdy posts, but it was easy to see and photograph from outside the fence. (Figure 8-2). The stone walls at Camlann weren't massively thick like those at Camelot; rather, they were constructed from stacked flat stones an inch or two thick and twelve to eighteen inches in diameter.

Figure 8-2 Ancient stone buildings unearthed at the Camlann archeological site.

In 1850, Archeological digs had turned up ancient weapons of war, including a battle axe, a spear, and a spur. These and other artifacts were displayed in an on-site exhibition room.

I continued across the fields until I saw a dense old forest with a trail leading to the River Camel. Nearby, tawny-colored, waist-high weeds grew in clumps around the field. I entered the forest and followed a twisting overgrown path for some time until I reached the river. The water itself wasn't particularly deep, but over millennia, it had carved a deep chasm in the rocks. In places, the riverbed lay six feet or more below the bank.

Somewhere along here, an army led by Arthur's son Mordred, had lain in wait to attack. The place was appropriately named Slaughterbridge. The outcome of the battle, well-known by now, was that Arthur prevailed and slew Mordred. But Arthur was wounded and subsequently died from his battle injuries.

I was not the first author to come here. On his visit to the site, Alfred Lord Tennyson wrote, "Camelford, Slaughterbridge, clear brook among the elders. Sought for King Arthur's stone, found it at last by a rock under two or three sycamores. The stone, a nine-foot pillar, lies in a dank picturesque setting by a stream. It is an inscribed memorial stone of the sixth century."

Long before Tennyson, Cornwall historian Richard Carew had, in 1602, located Arthur's Stone and recorded its Latin inscription. Even earlier, in 1136, Geoffrey of Monmouth had documented the field at Camlann as the site of Arthur's final battle in his *Historia Regum Britanniae*.

I followed the river's edge until I came to a sign bearing the legend of Arthur's Stone. Since Tennyson's time, the stone had slid down the riverbank and now lay at the water's edge, about nine feet below me. It was a solid gray stone that didn't look like a natural rock formation. Rather, it appeared to have been shaped by ancient craftsmen into a long rectangle, with evenly squared sides. Tennyson described it as a pillar, so at one time, it may have stood upright like a monolith. Its

Chapter 8 Camlann and Tintagel

Figure 8-3 Looking down on Arthur's Stone which lies on its side in the river.
Below: Close up of Arthurs stone showing inscribed lettering dated to 540 CE.

shape suggested to me that it might have once been an obelisk that was now missing its capstone.

Even from the top of the riverbank, I could clearly see the inscribed lettering, although a substantial amount of moss had grown on the stone. A sign nearby said both of the stone's two inscriptions had been dated to 540 CE. The sign also provided a translation of the Latin inscription: "Here lies the son of Mag-uri (Arthur the Great)." On another edge of the pillar was an inscription in an Irish script known as Ogham. Unfortunately, the runic text is now too damaged to be fully deciphered, but according to the sign, the legible portion appears to contain the same name.

I took several photographs of Arthur's Stone before my camera batteries died. Since I couldn't photograph any more of the site, I returned to the car and continued to Tintagel. There I bought fresh batteries and secured accommodation for the night at Pendrin Guest House, a tidy little bed-and-breakfast on Atlantic Road. There was a caravan camping park in a nearby meadow, and further down Atlantic Road, nearer to the ocean, sat a large building with a castle motif, turrets and all, named Camelot Castle. Of course, it wasn't Camelot at all, just a hotel so named to draw in tourists.

Figure 8-4 Pendrin Guest House in Tintagel.

My landlady told me it was owned by the Church of Scientology. That turned out to be false, but it would have been funny if true.

Tintagel Castle was about three-quarters of a mile from the guest

Chapter 8 Camlann and Tintagel

Figure 8-5 Front entrance to Tintagel Castle, reputed birthplace of King Arthur.

house—a fifteen- or twenty-minute walk to the entrance. The latter portion of the walk was down a steep hill, ending in front of a small café that sold tea and packaged sandwiches. I passed the café and entered the castle ruins through an ancient stone arch.

I climbed a series of stone walkways and steep steps to the main courtyard, which was hundreds of feet above the entrance. (Figure 8-6). The castle, built on a cliff above the Atlantic Ocean, had previously extended onto the adjoining Tintagel Island, where there was a second courtyard and another portion of the castle. The two parts of the castle had once been connected by a bridge that had since fallen. Yet I was able to photograph the island courtyard and castle ruins from where I stood.

Tintagel Castle's walls were not the twelve-foot thick battlements of Cadbury. Instead, they were only two-feet wide in most places, made from slabs of flat slate, a stone readily available from a slate quarry that had once existed not far from the castle entrance.

Figure 8-6 The two courtyards of Tintagel Castle as seen from above.

Thinking back to the Dark Ages and the medieval period, when castles and forts were built for defense, it was apparent why the Dukes of Cornwall had chosen this location. Hundreds of feet above the ocean's surface, it would have been nearly impossible to attack by sea. Invaders arriving by land would have had to first come down the long incline I had walked from town, then fight almost straight up steep crags before reaching the castle walls. The whole while, the invaders would be targets for archers from above. If defenses failed and the castle was breached, the occupants could have retreated to the island and raised the bridge.

So, why did I go to Tintagel? It all goes back to Geoffrey of Monmouth and his *Historia Regum Britanniae*, which claimed Tintagel Castle was Arthur's birthplace—not this specific structure, but an earlier one. That belief suited another Richard, the First Earl of Cornwall, who acquired the site in a land swap with Gervase de Tintagel in 1225. He attained the site to strengthen his connection to King Arthur, and also because it was the traditional seat of Cornish kings.

Chapter 8 Camlann and Tintagel

If a myth is strong enough, does it become true? The castle ruins in which I stood had been built in 1233 by Earl Richard. Historians initially debunked the story of Tintagel being Arthur's birthplace, because he was born in the late fifth century, before the castle was built. Still, the legend persisted. Then in the 1930s archeological excavations found that Richard had indeed built over an earlier site that dated far back into the Roman occupation—far enough that it could have existed during Arthur's time. The lesson: there's something behind Arthurian myths.

According to archeologist and historian Charles Thomas, the evidence showed that the site was inhabited prior to the Dark Ages by royals and their entourage. Finds of Roman coins and Mediterranean, African, and Phoenician pottery indicated that the previous occupants were substantial and wealthy. After the Romans withdrew in the early fifth century, Britain split into separate fiefdoms, each with its own king.

Beginning in 2016, five years of new excavations revealed Tintagel to be an important center for Mediterranean trade in the post-Roman era between 450 and 650 CE. Discovery of Merovingian glass, amphorae from the eastern Mediterranean, and high-end pottery suggested an urbane setting fit for royalty or a high-status family.

I left the courtyard and made my way out of the castle. Next, I descended a set of wooden steps leading to a rocky beach. On my right, a beautiful waterfall poured over the cliff and flowed down into the Atlantic. (Figure 8-7). On my left was the entrance to a large natural cave located beneath the Tintagel Island portion of the castle. This was Merlin's Cave, a key place in Arthurian legend. (Figure 8-8.)

The story goes that King Uther Pendragon had an eye for Igraine, the wife of Gorlois, Duke of Cornwall. So, while the duke was away, Uther visited the castle and Igraine ended up pregnant. The myth claims that Uther had Merlin change his appearance so Igraine thought he was her husband. But doesn't that sound like a convenient explanation for an adulterous wife? "Your Grace, how did I know? He looked just like you."

69

Figure 8-7 Waterfall next to Tintagel Castle.

CHAPTER 8 CAMLANN AND TINTAGEL

Figure 8-8 Merlin's Cave, beneath Tintagel Castle, at low tide.

Anyway, the legend says that after Arthur's birth at Tintagel, the duke wasn't too happy that the king had his way with his wife. So Igraine arranged for Merlin to meet her in the cave beneath the castle. There she gave him baby Arthur to take away and raise elsewhere.

I walked thirty or forty yards into the three-hundred-foot-long cave. Water two or three inches deep pooled between the large, smooth rocks that covered the cave floor. Stepping on the stones, I was able to go anywhere I wanted without getting my shoes wet. Daylight from the entrance reflected off the puddles and cave walls, casting a violet luminescence. The place felt magical indeed.

Another story claimed Merlin was imprisoned in the cave for a period by some force or foe. Since Merlin's cave is accessible only when the tide is out, one could get trapped until the next tide. But does that qualify as an evil force?

Taking no chances, I left the cave well ahead of high tide, climbed the stairs, and exited the castle grounds. A car service was offering rides back to town for £1.50. I looked at the steep uphill climb ahead of me and gladly paid the money.

I returned to my room, cleaned up, had a brief rest, and then went out for dinner. I found a pub that offered several vegetarian entrees. When I finished eating, I left the dining room and went into the pub, where I consumed several glasses of cider and ale made in the area. The cider was delicious but potent. It was made from fallen apples that are called "scrummies" in the local vernacular. Later, I used this fact in my novel, *Lancelot's Disciple*, the sequel to *Lancelot's Grail*.

I met a couple of interesting Englishmen in the pub, and we drank together and talked. The first was a photographer who was fixated on large-format film and derided digital photography. I had switched from film to digital some years before. He was a former computer programmer, as was I, so we changed the discussion from cameras to computers and politics until Ian Sanderson joined us.

Ian was a scientist in geophysics. He described his work and said that by using magnetic sensing equipment, he could locate and identify underground sites that were buried long ago. He said this was possible because fire changes the magnetic field. He could find brick structures or even places where primitive people had fire pits, but his method couldn't detect stone castle or fort walls because they appeared the same as natural rock formations to his equipment. He mentioned another method of finding stone buildings but didn't elaborate.

He also suggested that I should talk with historical re-enactors as research for my book because they put on a persona and speak from the perspective of a person from the historical period they represent. It was an excellent suggestion. Two of the guides at Glastonbury Abbey had done just that. Unfortunately, during the rest of the trip, I never visited another site that had re-enactors as guides.

By the time I left the pub for the B and B, I felt tipsy from too much cider and ale. Fortunately, I was walking, not driving.

Chapter 9
St. Nectan's Waterfall

The bed-and-breakfast I had chosen in Tintagel served a very filling vegetarian version of a full English breakfast. Author William Somerset Maugham, who spent a large part of his life in France, famously said, "To eat well in England you should have breakfast three times a day." In his opinion, breakfast was the only meal the Brits did well.

Traditionally, the full English breakfast starts with orange juice, cereal, and stewed or fresh fruits. Then, the main course consists of bacon, eggs, and sausages, accompanied by a broiled or grilled tomato, toast, marmalade, and tea or coffee. Sometimes the accompaniments also include baked beans, fried potatoes, mushrooms or onions.

In recent decades, the health food industry has created vegetarian substitutes for bacon, sausage and other meats. The Tintagel bed-and-breakfast was the first place I'd stayed that offered meat substitutes to guests. As a vegetarian, I usually have to ask for the bacon and sausage to be omitted and request that my eggs not be fried in lard or bacon grease.

On my last morning in Glastonbury, when I informed Daisy I was heading to Tintagel, she recommended that I see the waterfall at St. Nectan's Glen, near Trethevy, which is located within the civil parish of Tintagel. I had decided Daisy's recommendation would have to wait until after I'd seen Arthur's birthplace. Now, having seen it, I could afford a minor stopover on the way to my next destination, Salisbury.

Figure 9-1 Granite milestone of the Roman road in Trethevy. Photo: Nilfanion.‡

Chapter 9 St. Nectan's Waterfall

The small hamlet of Trethevy was not far from my bed-and-breakfast. The hamlet has few ancient records, but many interesting historical features.

A granite pillar milestone—which is inscribed with the Latin words: "For the Emperor Caesars our lords Gallus and Volusian" (who reigned from 251 to 253 CE) indicates that a Roman road once ran through Trethevy. Its existence adds weight to the theory that Tintagel was an important center for trade with the Mediterranean. (Figure 9-1).

The pillar, which is situated along the roadside outside St. Piran's Church, is believed to have been the site of a sixth-century monastic settlement. St. Piran was the patron saint of Cornish tin miners. He is said to have miraculously floated to Cornwall on a millstone after being cast out of Ireland during the Dark Ages. He reputedly lived to be 206 years old. In addition to the church, Trethevy is also home to St. Piran's Well, a curious beehive-shaped structure topped with an iron cross. Although the present slate structure is not that old, the well has been considered a holy site for centuries.

Figure 9-2 St. Piran's Well. Photo: Nilfanion.‡

Figure 9-3 Arthur's Quoit—capstone of a Neolithic tomb monument predating Arthur by several thousand years. Photo: Jim Champion.‡

As with other communities in southwest Britain, Trethevy also has a mythical link to King Arthur. Further north along the road, at its intersection with the lane to Trewethett Farm, is an ancient megalithic capstone of a Neolithic tomb or monument. Its entire flat roof consists of a single humongous stone that rests on upright standing stones. Constructed about the time Abraham set out for the Promised Land, it predates King Arthur by several millennia. Nevertheless, it is known as King Arthur's Quoit, and folktales claim he threw the massive stones there from Tintagel Island. It is possible that the ancient tomb might have been the site of some long-forgotten meeting or battle in which Arthur participated, thereby associating his name with the place. But folktales in which he executes feats of fantasy do nothing to convince skeptics that he was an actual person.

A real mystery, though, is the maze carved into the face of a rock behind Trethevy Mill. The carvings date back about four thousand years and are remarkably similar to carved mazes found in Crete.

CHAPTER 9 ST. NECTAN'S WATERFALL

However, I hadn't come to Trethevy see all these interesting things. I'd come to see St. Nectan's Kieve, the proper name for the waterfall in St. Nectan's Glen. The site was located a few miles southeast of town, down a one-lane road. Its namesake, St. Nectan, was a fifth century holy man who was born in Wales in 468 CE.

According to a twelfth-century manuscript found in Gotha, he was the eldest of Welsh King Brychan's twenty-four children. Upon hearing the story of the great hermit St. Anthony, Nectan was inspired to seek solitude and left Wales with his companions intending to settle wherever their boat landed. They ended up on the coast of Devon, at Hartland, where they took up residence in a dense forest for several years. Nectan also spent some time in Cornwall, where he had a hermitage above the waterfall I was on my way to visit.

However, stories seldom end well for saints. Returning to Devon, Nectan and his followers relocated to a remote valley with a spring. While living there, he helped a swineherd recover his lost pigs and, in

Figure 9-4 Path to St. Nectan's Kieve.

return, was gifted two cows that were later stolen. On June 17, 510, he found the robbers and attempted to convert them to Christianity. But the robbers attacked him, and one of them cut off Nectan's head. The story goes that Nectan picked up his severed head and walked back to his well before collapsing and dying. Upon seeing this, the man who killed Nectan went insane, but the other thief buried Nectan. From that time onward, miracles took place at Nectan's tomb and a considerable cult grew up around his shrine, which continued to be popular throughout the Middle Ages. Eventually, he was venerated by the Roman Catholic Church, the Eastern Orthodox Church, and the Anglican Church—a saint three times over.

St. Nectan's Kieve turned out to be another one of those places—like Camelot—where you left your vehicle in a car park, and then walked to the site. This walk was much longer. I walked several miles down a one-lane road to a path, then another mile or two up a wooded path to a gate. At the gate, a little tea shop charged £3.50 to walk down to the falls. I paid the fee, opened the gate, and descended a set of steep, wet stone steps that had a handrail in only some places.

Figure 9-5 Stone steps down to the waterfall.

Chapter 9 St. Nectan's Waterfall

Figure 9-6 St. Nectan's waterfall makes a ninety-degree turn. Hovering in the photo are mysterious globes of light.

The steps ended in a large glen, a catch basin for the falls. A shallow river about six feet wide carried water away from the falls. I found myself in a magical fairyland of ferns and tiny shrines of stacked stones. A flat stone the size of a dinner platter held a carved image of Mary holding a baby. A fallen tree formed a bridge spanning the river, and ferns grew from its bark. Then I saw the falls. (Figure 9-6).

I've seen many waterfalls, but never one like this. It fell fifty or sixty feet into a pool, where it turned ninety degrees and poured out through a giant circular hole in a rock formation, creating a second falls, this one about eight feet high. As I started photographing it, I witnessed an unexpected phenomenon.

When I'd paid my fee at the tea shop, I'd seen an information board with some letters and photos from previous visitors but didn't grasp what they were about until I photographed the falls and saw for myself. Whenever my camera flashed, it illuminated large floating spheres of light about the size of soccer balls. I checked my camera to see if there were water drops on the lens. None. I tried turning off the flash, but then I couldn't see the spheres of light. I turned the flash back on and began shooting from different angles in case my relative position caused the lens flare. No difference. Floating balls of light hovered between me and the waterfalls in every photo—and not one or two, but dozens! I thoroughly enjoyed the wonderfully mysterious, unexplained magical effect. No wonder Daisy had directed me here.

When I returned to the tea shop above the falls, I perused the letters and photos I'd previously ignored. Photographers from all over the world had captured images of the same phenomena I'd just seen. It wasn't a quirk unique to my camera or the angle of the sun at a particular time of day. I couldn't explain it, but I'd seen it, and I had a dozen photos for proof.

Although I didn't know it at the time of my visit, St. Nectan's Glen and Trethevy are only a short drive from Trevalga, home of St. Petroc, a saint who would figure in my sequel novel, *Lancelot's Disciple*. I hadn't planned the sequel yet, so I had no inkling that I would refer to St. Petroc in my next book. I did, however, use the idea of a fallen tree serving as a bridge in both novels.

Chapter 9 St. Nectan's Waterfall

Reluctant to leave, I had lingered at the foot of the falls. But once I was back in my car, I saw the hour of the day and knew I needed to move along. Salisbury was 150 miles away and I'd have to drive for hours on the slower British roads to get there. I had additional stops I needed to make along the way. First up was Camelford, where I'd finish photographing the battleground and archeological excavation sites I hadn't been able to capture when my camera batteries ran out the day before. With fresh batteries, I made a quick stop, took my pictures, and got back on the road.

Despite the extra time spent and having to walk miles to the site, my side trip to St. Nectan's Glen turned out to be entirely worthwhile.

Chapter 10
Bodmin Moor

My next stop was Bodmin Moor, an eighty-square-mile granite moorland in northeastern Cornwall. It has been inhabited since at least the Neolithic era when primitive peoples farmed the land. They built megalithic monuments and stone circles that are still on the moor today.

Considerable areas of the poorly drained moor form marshes that can dry out during hot summers. The rest is either rough pasture or overgrown with heather and other low vegetation. Numerous species of birds and wildlife share the moor with domestic cattle, sheep and ponies.

The moor is the source of a half-dozen of Cornwall's rivers. Within it are three man-made reservoirs in addition to Dozmary Pool, Cornwall's only natural lake.

Located about nine miles northeast of the village of Bodmin, Dozmary Pool is small, about thirty-seven acres. I drove around its perimeter, stopping to take photographs from several vantage points. I was interested in the lake because of its place in Arthurian legend.

Early in King Arthur's rule, he is said to have rowed out on the lake where he met with a lady who gave him his famous sword, Excalibur. At the end of his life, as he lay dying from battle wounds, he gave the sword to his trusted knight, Sir Bedivere, commanding him to return it to the Lady of the Lake. In my novel, *Lancelot's Grail*, Sir Bedivere

Chapter 10 Bodmin Moor

recounts to Frith how he crossed the marshes of Bodmin Moor to return the sword for his king.

Camera in hand, I stood at the edge of the road visualizing Bedivere's story.

According to legend, Sir Bedivere saw the Lady of the Lake's hand reach up out of Dozmary Pool and catch Excalibur as he threw it. (Figure 18-1). I may not have seen the Lady, but I took home numerous photos of the lake and the moor, which I used to help me write descriptions of the landscape in my sequel, *Lancelot's Disciple*.

Dozmary Pool is also the source of the River Fowy, which flows south from the moor, eventually forming the Fowey estuary and emptying into the English Channel at the Port of Fowey. In *Lancelot's Disciple*, Frith sails down the River Fowey on his way out to sea, and upon returning from his voyage, he wanders the wilds of Bodmin Moor.

Figure 10-1 Dozmary Pool on Bodmin Moor.

Farther along on my drive, I stopped at Jamaica Inn, also on Bodmin Moor. In the seventeenth and eighteenth centuries, Cornwall apparently had a lot of smuggling activity. English author Daphne du Maurier's 1930 stay at the inn inspired her to write a novel she titled *Jamaica Inn*. Set in 1820, the book tells the story of Mary, a twenty-three-year-old woman who, after her mother's death, comes to the remote Jamaica Inn to live with her aunt. Mary notices that the inn never has any other guests and is never open to the public. Soon, she discovers it is the base of operations for a murderous gang that runs ships aground, kills the sailors, and steals the cargo.

Figure 10-2 Jamaica Inn on Bodmin Moor, inspiration for a novel by Daphne du Maurier.

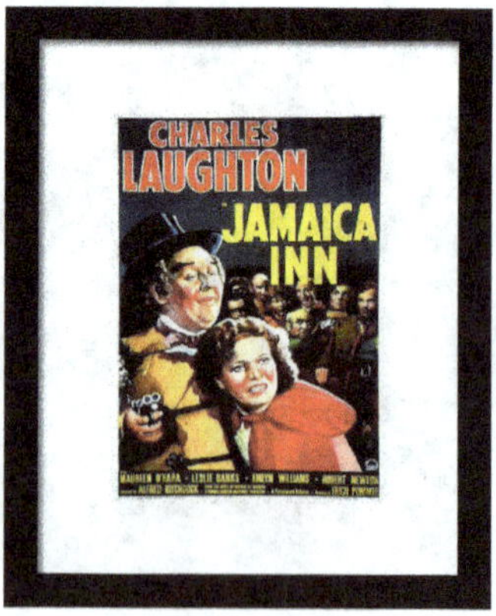

The book, a big success, was made into a film of the same name by Alfred Hitchcock, and later into a three-part BBC series that aired on PBS. Nowadays, the inn houses a pub and a museum about the book and movie. Although the museum was closed when I visited, the nearby pub was open. The whole place felt very touristy, and I didn't stay long.

Figure 10-3 Film poster.

Chapter 10 Bodmin Moor

I left the moor and continued toward Salisbury, which was still a long way off. I got on the motorway, a higher speed highway similar to a United States interstate. Unfortunately, I got confused by the road signs when I reached Exeter, and exited the motorway into busy city traffic. The good news was that I saved twelve pence a liter on gas.

It's easy for Americans to misunderstand European gasoline prices. I'd been paying $2.35 a gallon in the United States, so when I saw British stations advertising gas for £1.20, I thought, *what a bargain*. Then I learned that they sell it by the liter. Converting liters to gallons by multiplying times 3.78, that terrific price came to £4.53 a gallon—and that's British pounds, not dollars. So, not a great deal at all, but twelve pence in savings still saved me half a pound per gallon.

I refueled and found my way back onto the motorway. However, I didn't reach Salisbury until 6:30 p.m. I was tired by then, and I also had trouble finding a bed-and-breakfast. Several places had "no vacancy" signs, and another was too costly. Around dusk, I finally found a nice place that was affordable. Next, I focused on food. I walked to the center of town and ate a pizza.

By the time I finished eating and returned to the B and B, I saw it was almost time for the autumnal equinox, which would occur at 21:19 in England. I had come to Salisbury on this particular date because of its proximity to Stonehenge. I'd intended to drive out there that night to see if I could observe any special phenomenon or celestial alignment. Among the many theories about Stonehenge's purpose, most note its precise astronomical calculations of winter and summer solstices. I thought perhaps that included vernal and autumnal equinoxes, too.

Unfortunately, it wasn't meant to be. I'd taken too long to eat and could never drive there in time. I rationalized that since I was within a couple of miles of Stonehenge, any cosmic energy occurring there at the time of the equinox might extend throughout the area. So, I just meditated in my room at the designated time. But instead of finding some equinox phenomenon in my meditation, I found myself thinking.

I realized I'd been secretly hoping for an equinox experience similar to one I'd had in Colorado years before, about which I'd written the poem "Mountain Breathing" and published in a book of the same name. Back then, I'd followed a guide up a trail high in the Rockies. At an elevation of eleven or twelve thousand feet, we paused to rest and fell into a meditative state. I swear, I actually felt a shift between two seasons as distinct as dropping a weight on an old-fashioned balance scale. My guide said she'd felt the same phenomenon.

Figure 10-4 Poetry book by author.

It was also strange that on my last night in Tintagel, I'd seen an Englishwoman who reminded me of a woman I'd worked with during college who'd spent a semester abroad in Gloucester. I remembered a poem I'd written about her time there. Before leaving Tintagel, I studied the roadmap to see if my journey would take me near enough to Gloucester for a side trip. Funny how poems I wrote forty or fifty years earlier were suddenly coming to mind.

I shook off my distraction. We can never recreate the past. So, why did I want to? Here I was in England, just two miles from Stonehenge. Why ruminate about an experience on a Colorado mountain half a lifetime ago? Why think of chasing a poem to Gloucester? So far, every place on this trip had been exactly as it was supposed to be. I'd visit Stonehenge the next day.

Chapter 11
Salisbury and Old Sarum

Since I'd already missed visiting Stonehenge during the previous night's equinox, I figured there was no reason to rush out there first thing after breakfast. I'd been to the monument on previous trips to England and those rocks weren't likely to go anywhere anytime soon. On the other hand, I'd never been to Salisbury, so I might as well see some of it first. Then, on my drive to Stonehenge, I could also visit Old Sarum, a historic ruin.

I left my car at the B and B and walked to Salisbury Cathedral along the picturesque River Avon—a long, but pleasant stroll. The morning had warmed. Mute swans and mallard drakes swam in the water. (Figure 11-1). A beautiful brick bridge arched over the river, and I paused to take photographs. The river walk opened into St. Thomas Square—a veritable postcard market of quaint shops, their exteriors adorned with hanging baskets full of colorful flowers. (Figure 11-2). The square was paved with slate, and in the middle, pink, red, and white flowers grew in a centerpiece as large as my rental car.

On the far end of the square was one of several entrances to Salisbury Cathedral, a significant site for many reasons. Its eighty-acre cathedral "close," the area surrounding a cathedral that's owned and governed by the church, is the largest in England. The cathedral's massive stone structure also has the country's largest cloister. At 404 feet, the church's spire is Britain's tallest. And its medieval clock, which still chimes every quarter hour, is the oldest working model in the world.

Figure 11-1 River Avon in Salisbury, Wiltshire.

Chapter 11 Salisbury and Old Sarum

Figure 11-2 St. Thomas Square, part of the cathedral close.

Figure 11-3 Author standing in front of Salisbury Cathedral. Niches in the exterior hold statues of angels, apostles, philosophers, and others.

Chapter 11 Salisbury and Old Sarum

I should also mention that Salisbury houses the best-preserved of the four surviving copies of the Magna Carta. This important document became the symbolic foundation for modern English government and influenced the framers of the American constitution. On display for all to see was one of the original eight-hundred-year-old parchments.

One-hundred-thirty niches span the front of the cathedral and continue around the turrets. (Figure 11-3). Seventy-three of these niches hold statues of varying sizes arranged in five rows. The upper rows feature angels, archangels, Old Testament patriarchs, apostles, evangelists, martyrs, doctors and philosophers. On the bottom row stand statues of royalty, priests and worthy people with connections to the cathedral.

The cathedral is the subject of William Golding's novel, *The Spire*, and it's also the model for the fictional Kingsbridge Cathedral in Ken Follett's historical novel *The Pillars of the Earth*. Additionally, the cathedral is the subject of a famous painting by John Constable. Furthermore, Salisbury served as Thomas Hardy's setting for *Jude the Obscure*.

Salisbury has a nice museum as well. It features medieval paintings, glass, and embroidery; Tudor brass pieces, carving, and heraldry; and Georgian woodwork and wrought iron. After exploring the cathedral and museum, I returned to my car and proceeded two miles north of town to the site of Old Sarum, which is inextricably linked to Salisbury. In fact, the story of Sarum is the reason Salisbury exists at all.

At Old Sarum, I visited the ruins of an ancient castle and, next to it, the outlines of a huge cathedral. The castle site had been used by kings dating back hundreds of years before William the Conqueror.

A hill-fort since the Iron Age, and known in Roman times as Sorviodunum, Sarum was successively occupied by the Romans, the Saxons, the Danes, and finally, the Normans. Here, in 1070, within these very walls, William the Conqueror paid off his army and awarded the spoils of his 1066 invasion. In William's day, the fort's fortifications consisted of an outer defensive wall and an inner rampart that rose at a steep angle and measured forty feet from trough to top. Construction of the royal castle, in whose ruins I stood, had already been started by his chancellor. A vibrant town grew around the castle, which served as the residence of King William I and his successors for the next 220 years.

Figure 11-4 Surviving walls of the castle at Old Sarum where William the Conqueror rewarded participants in the Norman Invasion.

Chapter 11 Salisbury and Old Sarum

The cathedral at Sarum was also the predecessor of the one in Salisbury and was used until the twelfth century, when tension developed between church and state over secular versus ecclesiastical power. The disputes lasted for fifty years, until the bishop proposed to King Richard I that they move the cathedral away from the castle. Richard approved the plan and construction began two miles south.

The move had two results. First, the new cathedral was finished in just thirty-eight years. Other medieval churches took centuries to build, so they ended up as a mix of styles as architecture evolved. Due to its rapid construction time, however, Salisbury Cathedral was an exception and became a spectacular example of a single architectural style, Early English.

Figure 11-5 Salisbury Cathedral the only medieval church of a single architectural style.

The second effect was that the whole town of Sarum packed up and moved south, forming a new city around the new cathedral. With the population decimated, the kings eventually abandoned the use of Sarum Castle, too. Over time, the site was reclaimed by nature, and by 1500, Old Sarum had become pastureland.

In recent times, the ancient hill-fort, with its impressive Norman fortification, has been excavated and can now be appreciated for the important stronghold it used to be. This great ruin is often overlooked by tourists who are in a hurry to reach nearby Stonehenge. But as I walked the excavations and stood inside the outlines of stone-walled rooms, I was glad I'd stopped to see it.

Nine hundred years after the Norman Conquest, standing amidst Sarum's crumbled walls, I thought about an ancestor of my mother, Ivo de Taillebois, who rode at William's side. What must this place have been like in those heady days after William took the throne? Was this where Ivo received his reward, the Barony of Thornborough? Our family history doesn't specify where the king granted him land and a title, but Ivo could have been standing in this very courtyard.

Chapter 12
Stonehenge

Leaving Old Sarum, I proceeded to Stonehenge. Except for St. Nectan's Glen, my journey up to this point had followed my intention to visit the sites associated with King Arthur. But I added Stonehenge to my itinerary simply because it is expected that tourists make a pilgrimage to walk among the circle of gigantic stones.

I'm not sure if there is a formal trade agreement with Britain requiring it, but when I was returning to the United States once, the customs officer actually insisted I turn on my computer and show her that I had taken photos of Stonehenge.

When I'd visited the monument twenty years before, nothing had been there but the stones themselves. You could wander freely among them—even lie down on one if you wanted. This time was different. Now it felt like one of those museum exhibits where they only permit you to peer into a room of antiques over a velvet rope. Except these weren't fragile Louis XVI chairs. These were twenty-five-ton stone rectangles standing thirteen to twenty-four feet tall.

The National Trust had strung a knee-high rope around the entire circumference, so you couldn't get too close. Anyone could easily have stepped over it, but signs every so often said "Do not cross rope line."

Although an informational pamphlet claimed the rope line had been erected to minimize the impact of too many tourists tramping around, it omitted the fact that the UK had constructed a major road only a

Figure 12-1 Author standing next to the rope line at Stonehenge.

hundred yards from the site in addition to adding parking lots, gift shops, and ice cream stands.

Still, if you turned your back on all the commercialization, you stood before a monument steeped in magic and mystery. While it can't be said with absolute certainty what the ancients used it for, it is evident on first sighting that it wasn't constructed for any casual purpose. The site had weight and gravitas, no pun intended. Ten thousand years ago, Neolithic people began constructing a work so magnificent that even today, one is awed by it.

Archeological evidence suggests that as early as 8,000 BCE, long before stones were brought to the site, pine posts two-and-a-half feet in diameter were erected in an east-west alignment and remained in place until they rotted. Over subsequent millennia, ancient peoples continued developing the Stonehenge site, consistently positioning the monument's features along lines of celestial transit. One theory is that Stonehenge served as an astronomical observatory.

CHAPTER 12 STONEHENGE

Figure 12-2 In the foreground is the banked ditch that surrounds Stonehenge.

Around 5,000 years ago, Stonehenge was transformed with the addition of a circular enclosure 360 feet in diameter. From an airship or drone, neither of which were available to the Bronze Age builders, Stonehenge would appear as concentric rings formed by a ditch with an adjacent high bank on the inside and a low bank, or counterscarp, on the outside. The banks were constructed of Seaford chalk that came from the ditch as people dug it by hand, using picks made from antlers.

The circle shape had two entrances, a wide one at the northeast end and a smaller entrance at the south. A long processional avenue led to the larger entrance from River Avon, which was about two miles away. Archeologists have found evidence to suggest that some type of timber structure existed within the circular enclosure during this time period.

Of course, from ground level, the eye tends not to focus on the circular bank of the earlier Stonehenge, but on the most recognizable feature of this icon, the horseshoe-shaped ring of erect stones with its open end facing northeast. And foremost among Stonehenge's many mysteries is how its standing stones got here.

The stones are of two types: sarsen sandstone and bluestone, an igneous rock harder than granite. But there isn't a nearby source for either. About 4,400 years ago, Neolithic people erected the first standing bluestones inside the circular enclosure. The stones were quarried in Pembrokeshire, Wales, and transported 150 miles to Stonehenge. Theories about how they were moved to the Salisbury Plain from a quarry in Wales vary from human transport to flying saucers, with proof of neither.

A larger circle of bluestones once flanked the inner side of the enclosure's circular bank, but all that remains of that circle today are fifty-six evenly spaced holes, each about thirty-nine inches in diameter. English antiquarian John Aubrey discovered them in the seventeenth century and they've been called the Aubrey holes ever since. For centuries, they were believed to have held timbers that were used to hoist the standing

Figure 12-3 Computer image showing the arrangement of stones when Stonehenge was intact. Illustrator: George Bailey.†

Chapter 12 Stonehenge

stones we see at Stonehenge today. However, archeological excavations conducted from 2004 to 2009 revealed that the Aubrey holes once held standing bluestones.

Figure 12-4 illustrates an overhead view of Stonehenge: a ring 360 feet in diameter formed by a low bank, a deep ditch, and a high bank. Then, just inside the ring's perimeter, there is another circle formed by fifty-six evenly spaced bluestones, standing upright, each weighing from two to four tons. At the center of the monument stands another circle of bluestones that's thirty feet in diameter.

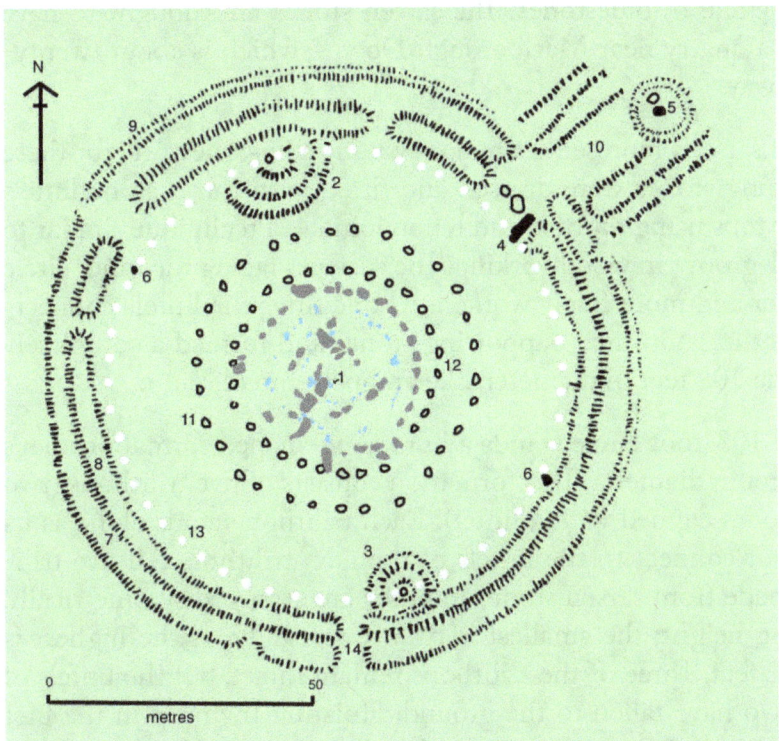

Figure 12-4 Birds-eye view drawing showing the location of banked ditches, posts, Aubrey holes, standing stones, and processional entrances. Illustrator: Adamsan.‡

Legend: 1. The Altar Stone, 2 & 3. Barrows (without burials) 4. The fallen Slaughter Stone, 5. The Heel Stone, 6. Two of originally four Station Stones, 7. Ditch, 8. Inner bank, 9. Outer bank, 10. The Avenue (a parallel pair of ditches and banks leading to the River Avon), 11. The Y holes (ring of 30 pits), 12. The Z Holes (ring of 29 pits), 13. The Aubrey holes (circle of 56 pits), 14. Smaller southern entrance.

It is interesting to note that the bluestones have acoustic properties and produce a ringing or a clanging bell sound when struck. I have read that some ancient cultures believed rocks that produced ringing tones possessed mystical or healing powers. This fits with another theory that Stonehenge was a place of healing—perhaps the Bronze Age equivalent of Lourdes.

Approximately five hundred years after the bluestones were installed, a third phase of development took place. Sarsen stones were brought to Stonehenge and erected in a circle that surrounds the aforementioned thirty-foot circle of bluestones. The sarsen stones are thought to have come from a quarry near Marlborough Downs, which is about twenty-five miles away.

This ring of sarsens represents a major evolution in stonework, for these thirty standing stones were dressed and fitted with thirty stone lintels across their tops using mortise and tenon joints—a technique similar to tongue-and-groove in woodworking. The surfaces facing the inner circle are smoother and more finely worked. At one time, the lintels connected to each other atop their supporting stones and formed a completely capped circle 108 feet in diameter, like an open-air coliseum.

Within the 108-foot circle stands a horseshoe-shaped formation that's forty-five feet in diameter. This formation consists of five trilithons (two standing stones capped with a lintel). Each trilithon stands alone as its lintels do not connect to the lintels of the next trilithon. All five trilithons are made from sarsen stone, and they are arranged symmetrically, in increasing height; the smallest is twenty feet tall and the highest is twenty-four feet. Three of the trilithons remain intact, but the lintels of the other two have fallen to the ground. Hoisting them up in the first place must have been quite a feat, for they weigh up to fifty tons each.

As marvelous an engineering achievement as its construction was for its time, and as magnificent as Stonehenge still appears to us today, it is in ruin compared to what it once was. Over the millennia, several of the lintel stones in the 108-foot ring have fallen, leaving gaps. Other stones were removed in previous centuries to be used for building construction.

Chapter 12 Stonehenge

Figure 12-5 Close up of standing stones trilithon. Each stone weighs up to fifty tons.

Four of the remaining stones contain Bronze Age carvings, but nature has taken its toll and the prehistoric carvings are weatherworn.

A big mystery is the precision with which the monument aligns to the sunrise of the summer solstice and the sunset of the winter solstice. Additional holes within the monument no longer hold stones or wooden timbers but seem arranged to predict lunar eclipses.

Although there are no graves inside Stonehenge, cremation remains and bone fragments were found in the Aubrey holes. This led to speculation that Stonehenge was a cemetery, but it seemed to me more likely that the monument had served as a ceremonial ritual site that was used prior to interring bodies in one of the 350 burial mounds on the Salisbury Plain outside of Stonehenge. Think of a modern-day church funeral. When the service is over, the body is taken out to the cemetery. While ashes and pieces of cremated bone were found in the Aubrey holes, that does not necessarily mean they were cremated there. Many religions consecrate a place by including relics in the foundation or altar. It would not be difficult to imagine Neolithic people sprinkling an important person's ashes into a hole as a bluestone was about to be set in place.

As I drove away, I thought back to King Arthur. Stonehenge existed long before his time, and though no battles or ceremonies in his legend link him with this place, he surely knew of it—the marker I saw on the summit of Camelot earlier in my trip had listed Stonehenge as one of the distant points that could be signaled from Camelot.

Whether any such signal was ever needed, and regardless of whether Arthur ever had reason to go there, I was glad I had taken time from my journey to revisit this surviving marvel of the Bronze Age. Whatever meaning this place had, it was so important that it was worth the tremendous effort to construct it, and its significance has continued for eight thousand years.

Chapter 13
Marlborough

Without a doubt, Stonehenge is the world's most famous prehistoric monument, but it is not the only henge. Throughout the Salisbury Plain are other Neolithic henges made of upright stone or timber. On the same plain are also several hundred burial mounds, long barrow tombs, and a cursus, which is another type of ancient monument. The cursus on Salisbury Plain is a large rectangular earthwork aligned east to west. Constructed 500 to 700 years before Stonehenge, it is almost two miles long, ranging in width from 330 to 490 feet.

The cursus is located about a half-mile from Stonehenge. I passed it while driving to Marlborough, where I planned to spend the night. I could easily see it from the car, so did not stop there. Cursus monuments are also found elsewhere in Europe, but as with this one, their function remains unclear, although it's believed to be ceremonial. In fact, this entire area of Britain is replete with Neolithic, late Neolithic and early Bronze Age monuments that ancient peoples created for ceremonial and funerary practices.

While driving to Marlborough, I also saw a giant white horse carved into a hillside. (Figure 13-1). When I say giant, I mean that you can see it from seventeen miles away. The figure was created by digging deep enough into the soil to expose the underlying chalk rock. I later learned that there are several of these horses carved at various locations throughout Wiltshire. The largest, near the village of Westbury, is 180 feet tall and 170 feet wide and situated just above an Iron Age fort. The

Figure 13-1 Giant white horse carved into the distant hillside by exposing the underground layer of chalk.

others are only slightly smaller. It is uncertain when they were created, but a horse figure northeast of Marlborough was dated to the late Bronze Age or the early Iron Age.

When I reached Marlborough, I was exhausted from all the walking I'd done in Salisbury and decided to quit the road early to find a B and B. This was another city in which it was tough to find lodging in my price range. Eventually, I found a city tourism office that secured me a room at the Orchard Close, a cute place hidden down a narrow alley called Wye Lane.

I took a nap and then walked to town for dinner. Marlborough's High Street is one of the widest in England. In places, it is as wide as a mall parking lot in the United States. I located a Thai restaurant with good food. The prices were high, but Thai is a dependable cuisine for vegetarians. I had intended to go out after dinner because Marlborough is a

Chapter 13 Marlborough

Figure 13-2 Marlborough High Street, one of the widest in Britain.

college town and looked fun, but I spent longer than I intended at the restaurant. Feeling tired, I decided to go back to my room.

The temperature was another factor in my decision. Up until that night in Marlborough, daytimes had been summery and the evenings had been warmer than I'd expected. But that night, it was chilly. Maybe the temperature had dropped as a result of the previous night's rain in Salisbury, or it felt colder simply because Marlborough was farther north. Fortunately, I had packed many warm clothes, anticipating that England would be cold, so I was prepared. But it didn't make sense to go out in the cold that night. Further exploration could wait until morning.

Legend claims that Marlborough's name comes from combining Merlin with an old English word for burial mound. Merlin, King Arthur's personal magician and advisor, is said to be buried here under a cone-shaped earthwork called Merlin's Mound. The tiered, man-made hillock stands sixty-two feet tall and is several hundred feet in diameter. It was long thought to have dated back to the sixth century, making it a plausible resting place for the old wizard. But radiocarbon tests on charcoal samples archaeologists took from the mound now indicate it was built about 2400 BCE, making it much too old to be his grave.

Whatever the truth, the mound is located on the college campus, which is private property, so I wasn't able to see it. I wasn't too disappointed, though, the main reason I had come to Marlborough was to visit Avebury, a little village to the west. Avebury was another Neolithic monument consisting of a stone circle even larger in diameter than Stonehenge.

While traveling to Avebury, I came to a road marker for the West Kennet Long Barrow, a 300-foot-long burial tomb built with sarsen stones and divided into chambers like medieval catacombs or a large modern-day mausoleum. It was found to contain the remains of forty-six individuals. I stopped the car and photographed it, but did not go in.

Figure 13-3 In the distance is West Kennet Long Barrow, a 300 foot long Neolithic burial tomb.

Chapter 13 Marlborough

Figure 13-4 Inside the entrance of West Kennet Long Barrow. Photo: Jarkeld.‡

On the eastern side of the same plain sits East Kennet Long Barrow, the largest long barrow in Britain. Fifty feet longer than West Kennet and is easily seen from the highway, it measures 350 feet long by 100 feet wide and 20 feet tall. The long barrows are thought to have been built between 3500 and 2500 BCE. While the East Long Barrow has yet to be excavated, we know sarsen stones support its burial chambers because due to erosion, they can be seen protruding at the south end.

From the West Long Barrow, Silbury Hill can be seen in the distance, another puzzle of prehistoric Britain. (Figure 13-5). Constructed over 4000 years ago, it is 130 feet high and its base covers an area of five-and-a-half acres. Silbury Hill is the tallest man-made mound in Europe. But it is not a burial mound. It is, in effect, an earthen pyramid. Despite many archaeological digs and an intensive investigation during the 1960s, its purpose remains a mystery. None of the excavations have revealed any remains or significant ancient artifacts. At least one archeologist believes Merlin's Mound in Marlborough to be a smaller cousin of Silbury Hill, as they share similar construction and were built during the same time period.

Figure 13-5 Silbury Hill, a Neolithic earthen pyramid.

Farther along the road, I also came upon an ancient obelisk built by prehistoric peoples and shaped like the Washington Monument in the United States, but there was no sign indicating its name.

Upon reaching Avebury, I discovered the National Trust was charging a hefty fee to park in its lot and walk through the stones, so I decided not to stop. But driving on, I turned the corner, and I found myself in the midst of the monument. Although the stones aren't as tall as those at Stonehenge, the stone circle is nearly three-quarters of a mile in diameter—large enough that the entire village of Avebury sits within the monument circle. (Figure 13-6).

Indeed, it was unnecessary to pay a parking fee to see the monument, for the stones were on every side of me and quite easily visible from the car. I slowed to a crawl and looked about.

Surrounding Avebury's circle of stones is a massive earthwork bank and ditch (the henge). One source estimated a million tons of earth had been moved to create it—a far larger project than Stonehenge.

Figure 13-6 Aerial view of Avebury surrounded by massive Neolithic earthwork bank and ditch. Photo: Detmar Owen.‡

Figure 13-7 The Avebury Stone Avenue, which is thought to be a processional path to a stone circle. Photo: Dick Bauch.‡

Unfortunately, many of the Avebury stones are now gone, having been taken in previous centuries to build houses, roads, or other projects. Still, enough stones are left to convey the site's importance to ancient peoples. A double line of stones, known as the Avenue, (Figure 13-7) intersects with the circle of stones at its southern edge. The Avenue is thought to have delineated a processional path to an additional stone circle monument, the Sanctuary, whose stones have since vanished—no doubt also stolen for construction. Another processional avenue led to the west side of the circle.

There are other man-made hills, mounds, henges, and sacred wells throughout the area surrounding Avebury. Taken together, the sites form a vast prehistoric complex, obviously intentionally arranged to serve some important ritual or purpose. The Salisbury Plain and Avebury area exemplifies the ancient peoples ability to plan, engineer, organize, and construct amazing monuments. Whatever the purpose of these structures, I couldn't help but be impressed.

* * *

Check-in for my return flight to the States opened at 5:00 a.m. on the morning following my trip to Avebury. The distance from Avebury to Bristol was reasonably short, but driving on the narrow English country roads could take a long time. To ensure I'd be on time for my flight, I made my way to Bristol and sought a B and B close to the airport. When I reached Bristol, I found myself in a traffic nightmare, bumper-to-bumper, stop-and-go traffic, for at least an hour. This affirmed my decision to look for accommodations near the airport. I found a place at an old farm.

I unloaded the car and headed back out, intending to go to the charming village of Bath for dinner. But getting to Bath involved driving through Bristol again. When I came to a huge traffic snarl and a sign warning of long construction delays, I changed my mind. I had seen Bath on a previous trip, and I could find some place to eat without fighting traffic, so

Chapter 13 Marlborough

I made a U-turn and returned to the B and B. I leisurely unpacked and re-packed everything for the next day's trip. Knowing I'd be sitting all day on the flight home, I took a long walk to stretch my legs. My walk took me past a nice English pub, where I ate dinner.

In the morning, I had no problem getting up because someone else at the B and B, who apparently had an early flight like mine, began moving around the place at 4:25 a.m. I looked at the clock and thought no reason to go back to sleep. I took a shower, meditated, skipped breakfast, and drove to the airport, where I returned the rental car. When I checked in for the short commuter flight from Bristol to Glasgow, the agent wouldn't allow my bag as a carry-on because of its size, although it would be the appropriate size for the larger plane from Glasgow to the United States. I pointed out that this was the same suitcase I'd flown in with, and a nice agent in Glasgow had gate-checked it for me. The woman wasn't persuaded and made me pay an extra £16 to have it sent in the luggage hold.

After the flight from Bristol to Glasgow, I had a long wait before I could check in for my flight to the States. Unfortunately, having to pay the luggage fee had left me with only enough English money for one coffee. Since I was leaving the United Kingdom in mere hours, I didn't want to exchange more dollars for pounds, so I hoped they'd serve a filling meal on the plane. They did, and the food wasn't bad.

Once I was home, I sorted photos of my trip into folders on my computer and typed up notes from my trip. I had tramped around Britain to get a feel for the area in which I had set my novel, *Lancelot's Grail*. I was satisfied with the results. I had a trove of photos and notes that allowed me to add accurate imagery to the book.

It took me several years to finish and publish *Lancelot's Grail*. While waiting for it to come out, I wrote a second novel, *Lancelot's Disciple*, for which my travel notes also proved useful in describing the areas where my protagonist walked in Britain.

Chapter 14
Reflecting on the King

Considerable time passed after the publication of my two Lancelot novels. Then one day, I re-read my travel journal, and decided to address whether King Arthur was a real person or a mythical character. Certainly, he has been the subject of many fantasy novels, and this might lead many Americans to think of him as we think of Paul Bunyan, purely a tall tale. But that isn't true in Great Britain, where Arthur is clearly regarded as a historical personage. The National Trust owns and protects historical sites associated with him. Universities devote archeological excavations to his battlefields, and the principal purpose of Geoffrey of Monmouth's text, *Historia Regum Britanniae*, was to delineate Arthur's lineage through to the kings of the twelfth century.

Geoffrey was neither the first nor the last to use Arthur's story for vested interests. King Arthur might be considered one of the most misused figures in historical references. His life and deeds have been claimed by various countries, kings, clerics, and scholars to perpetuate their own ends.

As English author Joseph Ritson wrote in 1825:

> No character, eminent in ancient history, has ever been treated with more extravagance, mendacity, and injustice than the renowned Arthur, the illustrious monarch and valiant commander of the Britons.

Chapter 14 Reflecting on the King

There is no doubt in my mind that the stories of Arthur and his knights became exaggerated over time, but we've done the same in the United States with our own heroes. Take, for example, America's first president, George Washington, whose actual achievements have been enhanced with stories about his chopping down a cherry tree or throwing a silver dollar from one side of the Potomac River to the other. Also consider that Arthur died almost 1500 years ago. If the United States survives another 1250 years, what further exaggerations might be added to Washington's legend?

Of course, the principal difference between these two heroes is the lack of written records about Arthur. While George kept over 1,400 letters from the American Revolutionary War, and thousands of articles were published about him during his lifetime, this was not the case for King Arthur. A little problem called the Dark Ages intervened, creating a scarcity of written records and a reversion to oral history. In fact, only four documents have been found that were written during the Dark Ages about the period of British history during which Arthur lived. All four were written centuries after his death, and the latter three are derivative of the first. I'll discuss those later. First, let's understand why there aren't better records.

The idea for my novel *Lancelot's Grail* came to me one weekend while I was watching a television documentary about Camelot. A second PBS show airing that same weekend also inspired the story. It concerned climate change and described a scientific study published by David Keys in 2000. He'd examined tree ring growth patterns as revealed in the grain of ancient Irish oak planks and identified a two-year period during which the sunlight was too poor to grow plants. Expanding his search to other parts of the globe, he found that this sudden climatic change had occurred worldwide and postulated it was brought on by a massive volcanic explosion in 535 CE, which precipitated a two-year period of darkness.

This meant that "Dark Ages" wasn't just a label for a time when civilization took a giant step backward; it was literally a period that began in darkness, and humanity required centuries to recover. Keys postulated

113

that this sudden climatic change brought droughts and famines, causing numerous kingdoms across the globe to collapse—he listed Camelot among them. That caught my attention, and I made people's superstitious reactions to the sun being blotted out a factor in my characters' isolation.

With few written records being produced during this time, history reverted to being passed down orally in folklore and poetry over the subsequent 500 years. So it's not surprising that Arthur's factual story was lost. A second factor, although later, was Henry VIII's dissolution of the monasteries. Monastery libraries and scriptoriums were vital repositories of ancient manuscripts. Whatever scraps of information they may have held about Britons prior to the Dark Ages were undoubtedly lost in the sacking and burning.

The road back to literacy was a long one. Only two early records documenting Britain's fifth- and sixth-century history are known to exist: Gildas's *De Excidio Britanniae* and Bede's *Historia ecclesiastica gentis Anglorum*. Three hundred years went by before an unnamed monk in Wales wrote about Arthur in *Historia Brittonum*.

Before exploring these texts, it's helpful to know what occurred in Britain prior to the Dark Ages. Rome conquered and occupied Britain in 43 CE. Then, in about 410 CE, Roman troops withdrew to protect Rome. Britain was left with many small realms, each with its own king or prince. With Roman forces gone, Germanic tribes began invading and occupying Britain. A leader of the Britons pulled together peoples of the various realms. Throughout history, it has been said that Arthur was that leader.

Since Arthur's forces were derived from other nobles and kings, his style, unlike later kings, was not to declare himself ruler over them, but to serve as the leader of their combined force. A telling indicator of this can be found in *Historia Brittonum*. The author writes: "In those days Arthur fought *with* the kings of the Britons against them [the Saxons] but he himself was the *dux bellorum*." Scholars note that "dux" identifies him as "leader in battles" alongside the kings, not "rex" (king) over them.

Chapter 14 Reflecting on the King

Two things seem certain about Arthur. He was a Briton (not Celt, Pict, Scot, or Saxon), and he was a Christian. As I learned on my trip, the first Christian church in Britain was established in Glastonbury in 63 CE, during the Roman occupation. In 313 CE, Emperor Constantine issued the Edict of Milan, which accepted Christianity, and ten years later, it became the official religion of the Roman Empire and its outposts such as Britain and Gaul. But in the five-hundred-year interval between Arthur's death and the Norman Conquest, other Celtic stories were mixed into Arthur's legend—and magic and Celtic goddesses seeped into the myths. Clearly these are additions.

In my opinion, Arthur's legend is based on a real person. But without any surviving writings from his lifetime, and with nothing written of him until centuries after the fact, we can't be certain. That said, it seemed responsible to read up on the few ancient documents to support my opinion. Fellow author, Ken Campbell loaned me numerous books on the subject, and I dove into a year-long study.

Chapter 15
A Dearth of Dark-Age Documents

Before writing this chapter, I reminded myself that I had not traveled to England to either validate or disprove King Arthur as a historical person. My goal was to visit sites in Britain where I could collect sensory impressions for my book on Lancelot.

I am not an academic historian, nor do I wish to engage in intellectual debate with scholars who have spent years dissecting, deconstructing, and analyzing the few surviving Dark Ages documents concerning Arthur.

While conducting my research, I waded through *King Arthur Myth-Making and History* by N. J. Higham. It is a tedious, heavily footnoted, study of other scholars' interpretations of the handful of sixth- to tenth-century documents in which Arthur is or isn't mentioned.

The problem that all scholars of the period face is that only four relevant manuscripts exist from the five-hundred-year Dark Ages period.

The earliest surviving work recounting Britain's history during and after the Roman occupation was written by Gildas, a sixth-century monk. His *De Excidio et Conquestu Britanniae*, which translates as *On the Ruin and Conquest of Britain*, is not an objective chronicle but a sermon blaming Britons for their dire state of affairs. His work is biased with moral lessons intended to whip sinners into shape. In a manner reminiscent of

Chapter 15 A Dearth of Dark-Age Documents

Figure 15-1 Statue of Saint Gildas near the French village of Saint-Gildas-de-Rhuys. Photo: Romary.‡

Old Testament prophets, he alludes that God allowed pagan Saxons to take the Britons' land in retribution for their moral failures.

At the time he was writing, Anglo-Saxons controlled Kent, Lincolnshire, Norfolk, Suffolk, the Isle of Wight, and the coastal areas of Northumberland and Yorkshire. The Britons still controlled the rest of the former Roman Britain.

As a history, Gildas isn't all that helpful. He provides historical details only if they serve his message and omits those that do not contribute to it. The document is consistently vague about names and dates. Then again, he was aiming at his contemporaries, not creating a record for posterity. Historians value this text because they believe it was written sometime in the 540s, making it the closest written account to the period being described.

Assuming the date of composition is accurate, that puts it in the decade following the fall of Camelot and the volcanic eruption David Keys identified. Hunger and plague are among the misfortunes Gildas names as God's vengeances on the people. Keys identified both as outcomes of the two-year loss of sunlight.

Scholars, looking to prove Arthur is a mythic figure, jump on the fact that Gildas never mentions him by name. However, their opponents point out that, for the most part, he only names the five kings he berates and makes no comments about kings in the other British kingdoms that existed at that time. Besides, Arthur would have already been dead by 540, and since he repelled the pagan Saxons, Gildas had no reason to rail against him.

The one other king Gildas mentions is the Romano-Briton Ambrosius Aurelianus, a war leader who won an important battle against the Saxons late in the fifth century. After a disheartening loss to the Saxons, Aurelianus pulled together the survivors and achieved the first military victory over the Saxon invaders. In the succeeding years, the Britons continued to battle the Germanic invaders.

Aurelianus's feats sound a lot like Arthur's, and some people think his name does, too. It has been suggested that over a lengthy period of oral history, the name Aurelianus might have morphed into Arthur. However, as I read further, subsequent writers incorporated Aurelianus into their versions of history by portraying him as Arthur's uncle or king.

Okay, that was Gildas's version, which used the British-Saxon conflicts as cautionary tales to browbeat his flock to a higher morality. Bede, an English Benedictine monk at a monastery in Northumbria—at that time a kingdom of the Angles—wrote another document that covered this same historical period. His *Historia ecclesiastica gentis Anglorum*, or *An Ecclesiastical History of the English People*, was completed in 731. Covering a broader time span, it begins with the arrival of the Romans, gives a brief account of Christianity in Britain, and then moves on to St. Augustine bringing Christianity to the pagan Angles and Saxons in 597. The book continues up through the 730s, providing a history of pagan versus Christian kings until all of England is finally converted.

Chapter 15 A Dearth of Dark-Age Documents

Figure 15-2 Venerable Bede writing his *Ecclesiastical History of the English People*.

Bede, writing two-hundred years after Arthur, draws on Gildas for information about that period. Like Gildas, Bede does not specifically refer to Arthur. However, he does provide expanded information on Ambrosius Aurelianus, which he gleaned from other resources. Bede wrote to please the English king of Northumbria, and his main complaint about the Britons is their failure to assist St. Augustine in converting the Anglo-Saxons. He's also miffed about the date when British Christians celebrate Easter.

After Bede, another hundred years passed before an anonymous Welsh monk compiled *Historia Brittonum*, circa 829–830. The new work drew heavily from Gildas and Bede, but was the first to identify King Arthur. In fact, it devotes several chapters to him. It also includes Ambrosius Aurelianus, thus creating a distinction that they were two different men. *Historia Brittonum* became the source for Arthurian stories that were later repeated and amplified by subsequent authors.

The next document is the *Annales Cambriae* (*The Annals of Wales*). Although the earliest existing version is a handwritten copy made in the twelfth century, the original is thought to have been created sometime between the years 954 and 970. Two entries in this text reference Arthur. One includes the battle at Camlann where Mordred died and Arthur fell. Another passage mentions Arthur and Merlin.

Then in 1066, the Norman Conquest happened. It took six years for things to settle down and William I to secure his throne. After the death of William and his successor, King Henry I, the country entered a period of anarchy. This kingdom of British, Anglo-Saxon, and now Norman kings, needed a clearly delineated account of British history. Enter Welsh monk, Geoffrey of Monmouth, whose parents may have been among the many Bretons who took part in the Norman Conquest and settled in the southeast of Wales. Bretons were Britons who had emigrated and settled in the part of northern France that we now call Brittany. At that time, the Romans referred to France as Gaul and Brittany as Armorica.

Geoffrey created *Historia regum Britanniae*, a twelve-book chronicle of the Kings of Britain and much of everything subsequently written about Arthur was derived from the last six books. The work suited the needs of the new Anglo-Norman kings, giving them a predecessor of heroic proportions.

Figure 15-3 Statue of Geoffrey of Monmouth. Photo: Colin Cheesman.‡

Chapter 15 A Dearth of Dark-Age Documents

Figure 15-4 Stained-glass window showing William of Malmesbury. Photo: Adrian Pingstone.

Preceding Monmouth's work by a decade, a monk in Wiltshire, William of Malmesbury, wrote *Gesta Regum Anglorum* (*Deeds of the English Kings*). He admitted he'd consciously patterned it on Bede's *Historia Ecclesiastica*, but his book included Arthur as a historical figure where Bede's had not. It is reputed that Geoffrey of Monmouth incorporated William of Malmesbury's history into his own work.

Here is a translation of a relevant passage from Malmesbury's *Gesta Regum Anglorum*:

> On the death of Vortimer, the strength of the Britons grew faint, their diminished hopes went backwards; and straight-way they would have come to ruin, had not Ambrosius, the sole survivor of the Romans, who was monarch of the realm after Vortigern, repressed the overweening barbarians through the distinguished achievements of the warlike Arthur.
>
> This is the Arthur about whom the trifles of the Britons rave even now, one certainly not to be dreamed of in false myths, but proclaimed in truthful histories—indeed, who for a long time held up his tottering fatherland, and kindled the broken spirits of his countrymen to war. At last,

at the siege of Mount Badon, trusting in the image of our Lord's Mother which he had sewn on his armor, rising alone against nine hundred of the enemy; he dashed them to the ground with incredible slaughter.

I found a connection between my journey and William of Malmesbury when I learned that he had been friends with the Abbot of Glastonbury, stayed at the abbey for some time, and wrote *On the Antiquity of the Glastonbury Church*.

Meanwhile, Arthurian stories had become staples of Welsh poetry and moved onto the Continent, gaining popularity in France. Poet Chrétien de Troyes entertained his patroness Marie, daughter of King Louis VII, with Arthurian stories. His source for these tales may have been Breton storytellers. In any case, his works introduced Lancelot, Percival, Yvain and others, further spreading Arthur's legend.

Figure 15-5 Engraving considered to be Chrétien de Troyes in his work studio.

As discussed in Chapter 5, monks at Glastonbury Abbey uncovered an ancient grave containing a leaden cross with an inscription that translates as: "Here lies interred the famous King Arthur on the Isle of Avalon."

After the discovery of this ancient grave, Arthurian legend became a tool of kings. In 1278, King Edward I and his queen presided over the relocation of Arthur and Guinevere's remains into a more prestigious marble tomb. When Edward III ascended to the throne, he announced plans to revive the Order of the Round Table.

The next king, Edward IV, shored up his contested claim to the throne by asserting his lineage from Arthur using Geoffrey of Monmouth's *Historia regum Britanniae*.

It was during Edward IV's reign that Sir Thomas Malory wrote his classic *Le Morte d'Arthur*, the best-known work of Arthurian literature. Mallory gathered and translated Arthurian stories from French prose and compiled them with English sources such as Geoffrey of Monmouth, to create a massive volume. Completed shortly after the invention of the moveable type printing press, it was published in 1485 and became wildly popular.

Since the time of its first publication, Malory's book has served as a resource for every author writing any story about Arthur or his knights, including yours truly. But Malory was no historian, and he made no effort to separate folktales from verifiable events. He was also a man of the fifteenth century and tended to portray castles and towers as they looked during his lifetime rather than detailing the cruder hill-forts that would have existed during Arthur's time, such as the one I saw at Cadbury/Camelot.

Figure 15-6 William Caxton published *Le Morte d'Arthur* in 1485.

While *Le Morte d'Arthur* assembled and preserved every scrap of lore about Arthurian times, Malory's inclusion of fictionalized plot elements and his careless approach to historical accuracy, probably set in motion centuries of subsequent arguments over whether Arthur was a historical figure or a myth.

Although Arthur remained a popular subject for readers, academic scholars spent the next four hundred years deconstructing, analyzing, and debating the handful of existing writings covering the "Arthurian period." These were primarily the Gildas, Bede, William of Malmesbury texts, and *Annales Cambriae*. Examining and comparing various manuscripts and translations, different scholars wrote papers arguing for or against a historical Arthur.

Then the twentieth century brought new information into the equation. Archeological digs began to find evidence of historical sites exactly where legends said they should be. New technologies dated discovered artifacts to the right period, and accurately dated versions of ancient manuscripts.

In 1998, a stone found at the Tintagel excavation site had the name "Artognou" written on it. This, of course, set off speculation that it referred to King Arthur.

Despite mounting physical evidence, academics continued to debate Arthur's historicity, but even the opposition threw him an occasional bone, as illustrated by the following quotation from nineteenth-century historian Edward Freeman:

> Most likely there was such a man [as Arthur], but we can tell nothing about him for certain. Some of the Welsh Kings are spoken of in our [Anglo-Saxon] Chronicle, but there is nothing there about Arthur, and the Welsh writers who speak of him did not write till long after. It is said that he won a great battle over the English at Badbury in Dorsetshire in 520, and that he was buried at Glastonbury. This is not unlikely, as there can be no doubt that Glastonbury was a great church in the Welsh times before the English came. And it is quite certain that the West-Saxon King did not conquer any part of Somersetshire till after the time when Arthur is said to have lived.

Arthur's transition from a historical figure to mythical figure took millennia, much of it driven by religious manipulation, and whether Britons, Anglo-Saxons, Normans, or Tudors were on the throne.

Chapter 15 A Dearth of Dark-Age Documents

Having visited many Arthurian sites myself, here are my answers to a few concluding questions.

Was Arthur a real person?
If you are a tourist visiting Britain today, the answer is a resounding yes.

Did a leader arise in the wake of the Roman withdrawal to recruit disparate clans for the purpose of fighting off invading Germanic forces and then organize a sort of united front?
Certainly.

Did Arthur die from wounds received battling Mordred for control of the kingdom?
Most likely.

Did his second, much younger wife have an affair behind his back with his best knight?
Could be.

Did he, as a young boy, possess the strength to pull out a sword embedded in stone?
Probably no more likely than George Washington chopping down a cherry tree.

Ah, but stories of Arthur and his knights have fascinated us for fifteen hundred years and will continue to do so. Tracing King Arthur through Britain was a trip worth taking.

Chapter 16
Enter the Knights

Of course, I didn't travel to Britain to write about King Arthur. My novel was going to be about Sir Lancelot after the fall of Camelot. I already had my story in mind and knew a good deal of background on Lancelot thanks to Sir Thomas Malory's *Le Morte d'Arthur*.

Figure 16-1 The 1893 edition of Thomas Mallory's *Le Morte d'Arthur*. Illustrator: Aubrey Beardsley.

Authors, like me, who have mined Arthur's legend for their own fiction, owe everything to Malory. He compiled all the Arthurian oral histories and set them down in eight books, which were later divided into twenty-one books. Historically accurate or not, his work remains the best original source from which all subsequent books and novels on Arthur and Camelot have been derived.

Stories of Sir Lancelot and his fellow knights

Chapter 16 Enter the Knights

existed long before Malory published them in 1485. Twelfth-century French poet, Chrétien de Troyes, composed lengthy poems about Lancelot and Guinevere, Erec and Enide, Percival and the Grail, and knight-errant, Yvain. Chrétien wrote most of these for his patroness Marie of France, Countess of Champagne, daughter of King Louis VII and Eleanor of Aquitaine. The Percival poem is the exception, which he dedicated to Philip I, the Count of Flanders.

Chrétien was vague about his source materials. Some names he used came from Geoffrey of Monmouth, but Lancelot was not mentioned

Figure 16-2 Lancelot crossing the Sword Bridge, from *Lancelot, the Knight of the Cart* by Chrétien de Troyes.
Illustrator: Atelier d'Evrard d'Espinques.

in *Historia regum Britanniae*. Likely sources may have also included Breton folklore, which may have accompanied a second migration of Britons to Gaul following the Anglo-Saxons' invasion of Britain.

Britons in Cornwall and Wales maintained regular contact and trade with their countrymen across the English Channel, and also shared their stories. This helps to explain how King Arthur and his knights became popular subjects in France.

Undoubtedly, Chrétien was one of the sources Malory incorporated into his books. Chrétien's Percival also inspired the German stories of Parzival. But while Chrétien's other knights might have come from Briton, Breton, and Celtic lore, Percival most likely was inspired by the tale of a Tuscan saint, Galgano, a knight struck by a vision of God.

Aside from his connection to Percival, I noticed the name Galgano is visually similar to Galahad, a knight who brings a visionary experience of God to King Arthur's court in Malory's telling. Saint Galgano is known to have plunged a sword into the ground, where it became fused with the rock such that no one could remove it. The actual sword in the stone can be seen at the Chapel of Montesiepi in Tuscany, Italy. But Malory repurposes the "sword in the stone" story multiple times, with different characters, throughout *Le Morte d'Arthur*.

Although I've made the case for Arthur being a real person, nothing beyond folk legend suggests a historic Lancelot. One of the foremost authorities on medieval and Arthurian literature believes that Chrétien could have derived the name Lancelot from the Irish character Llenlleog or the Welsh hero Llawwynnauc. These two could, in fact, be the same figure as they both wield a sword and fight for the same cause in their respective Irish and Welsh tales. Since Chrétien acknowledged using Monmouth as source material, another theory is that Lancelot is a variation of Anguselaus, whom Monmouth mentions.

Although Lancelot may not have been a historical person, he is a "historical literary figure" embedded in practically every Arthurian story written since 1150. Lancelot is best known for his adulterous affair with Queen Guinevere. But that story, too, may have evolved from French

Chapter 16 Enter the Knights

poems about Tristan, Isolde, and King Mark, written by Thomas of Britain and Breton poet, Béroul, who wrote a Norman language version.

In both stories, the hero knight rescues a damsel who has been imprisoned in another land by an evil kidnapper whom the knight defeats. In Tristan's case, he travels to Ireland to bring Isolde back so she can marry his uncle, Mark of Cornwall. On the way, Tristan and Isolde ingest a love potion that causes them to fall madly in lust.

With Lancelot and Guinevere, she is already queen by the time he rescues her from being kidnapped. But there is a delay in returning her home and they spend the night together. Things are never the same between them after that.

Following a standard medieval motif of courtly love, Tristan, King Mark, and Isolde of Ireland, all love each other. Tristan honors and respects King Mark as his mentor and Mark loves Tristan as he would a son. Mark loves his wife, and Isolde is grateful that he is kind to her, but she and Tristan can't keep their hands off each other.

Arthur is considerably older than Guinevere, who is his second wife—a real May-December arrangement. Arthur loves her and also loves Lancelot, whom he calls his greatest knight. Although he turns a blind eye to the hijinks going on at Camelot, he repeatedly sends his knights out on quests, conveniently getting Lancelot away from his wife.

Tristan's uncle eventually learns of his nephew's affair with Isolde and seeks to entrap the couple. When King Mark acquires what seems to be proof of the lovers' guilt, he resolves to hang Tristan and burn Isolde at the stake, but he sticks her in a leper colony instead. On the way to the gallows, Tristan escapes and rescues Isolde. They take shelter in a forest where Mark discovers them. Then, they make peace. Tristan promises to return Isolde to Ireland and leave Britain. After doing so, he travels to Brittany, where he marries another woman who is, coincidentally, named Isolde.

In Arthurian legend, the end of Guinevere's affair starts similarly. Arthur's nephew, Mordred, exposes her affair with Lancelot in an effort to instigate a civil war, but Arthur refuses to burn Guinevere or cast her out. First of all, she brought to the marriage a dowry of one hundred knights to add to his forces. Second, he's established a code of chivalry and feels bound to defend her honor. Third, he recognizes Mordred's chicanery as an attempt to seize the throne, and thus meets him in battle.

Unlike King Mark, Arthur dies from battle wounds. Guinevere enters a convent, and when Lancelot comes to see her, she sends him off to become a religious hermit. The fact that their story might have been derived from Tristan and Isolde didn't bother Malory a bit. He resolved the question by including both couple's stories, treating them as separate incidents involving different people.

Then again, perhaps kings being cuckolded by their wives did happen more than once. Certainly, that was the situation with Arthur's parents, which I learned when I visited Tintagel. Consider the striking resemblance of these couples to the tenth-century Irish tale, *The Pursuit of Diarmuid and Gráinne*. Fionn, the aging leader of a warrior band, becomes engaged to a young princess named Gráinne after his first wife dies. At the betrothal ceremony, Gráinne is put off by how old her intended is, and she becomes irresistibly attracted to Fionn's best warrior, Diarmuid. With skillful persuasion, she convinces Diarmuid to run off with her. Initially, he refuses to have sex with her out of loyalty to Fionn, but he must not have held out for too long because she soon becomes pregnant. Her foster father negotiates a peace with Fionn, who later invites Diarmuid to a boar hunt during which Diarmuid is gored and dies from the wound.

Whether these are the same stories with different character names and details or coincidentally similar results of human foibles, none of the couples end up living "happily ever after."

Despite the similarity of these stories, Chrétien's romance poems provided the most important contribution—examples of the ideals of chivalry. These ideals became ingrained in Arthurian legend and survived as the code of conduct for knights well into Malory's time.

Chapter 16 Enter the Knights

Geoffrey of Monmouth defined the code as an oath a knight took to "never do outrage or murder and always to flee treason and give mercy unto him that ask of mercy and always to give gentle ladies and women succor upon pain of death."

In addition to Chrétien, Wace was another French poet who fed the growing fascination for Arthurian stories. Wace was a contemporary of Chrétien, but wrote in the Norman language. Like Chrétien, Wace mined Geoffrey of Monmouth's *Historia regum Britanniae* and produced *Roman de Brut*, a 14,866-line poem covering the history of Britain and King Arthur.

Wace is the first author to mention King Arthur's Round Table. Now, if Arthur was an authentic historical figure, the principal idea of the Round Table makes sense. Since Arthur's main forces were derived from those of other nobles and kings, the legendary Round Table would be a savvy move on Arthur's part. By giving each fiefdom equal prominence in his court, he ensured their cooperation against invading armies. Wace claimed he did not make up the idea of the Round Table but rather learned of it from Bretons.

Figure 16-3 Illustration of Wace presenting his *Roman de Rou* to Henry II. Illustrator: Frédéric Pluquet.

Figure 16-4 Henge known as Arthur's Table located in Eamont Bridge, Cumbria, England. Photo: David Mathews Lyons,†

One of the places I did not visit when I toured Britain was a Neolithic henge named King Arthur's Round Table. Like at Stonehenge and Avebury, a banked ditch defines the henge's circumference of King Arthur's Round Table. Unlike the henges on Salisbury Plain, there are no standing stones at the center of this monument. Instead, it is a large, round, flat formation about 165 feet in diameter. A photo of the henge (Figure 16-4) brings to mind a giant round dining table—hence, its name. However, being located three-hundred miles northwest of Glastonbury, it doesn't seem like a convenient meeting place.

Another Round Table, around which King Arthur's knights most assuredly did not congregate, hangs in the Great Hall of Winchester Castle. This table was constructed from English oak in 1290 for a Round Table tournament celebrating the betrothal of one of King Edward I's daughters. At eighteen feet in diameter, it's considerably smaller than the henge version, but it's no lightweight. It tips the scales at just over 1.3 tons, so hanging it must have been a challenge. (Originally, the table had legs and stood on the floor as one would expect.)

Chapter 16 Enter the Knights

Figure 16-5 King Arthur's Round Table at Winchester Castle created in 1290 to celebrate the betrothal of a daughter of King Edward I. Photo: R. S. Nourse.‡

Around the Winchester Round Table are places for twenty-four knights to sit, each bearing the name of one of King Arthur's knights. These were probably added when King Henry VIII had the table decoratively painted in 1522, perhaps inspired by Sir Thomas Malory's story of the Siege Perilous.

One of the key events in *Le Morte d'Arthur*, the lead-in to the quest for the Holy Grail, is Sir Galahad's arrival at King Arthur's court. As Malory tells it, every seat at the Round Table is inscribed with the name of a knight, except one. At the Siege Perilous, the inscription warns that if anyone other than a true Grail knight sits in that spot, he will be instantly struck dead. No one wants to chance that, so the seat remains vacant.

Figure 16-6 Illustration of Sir Galahad brought to the table of King Arthur's Pentecost feast. Illustrator: Walter Crane.

Then, one year, King Arthur holds a banquet to celebrate Pentecost. The arriving guests are surprised to find the inscription at Siege Perilous has changed to read: "It is time for the seat to be filled." While they marvel over this miracle, an old man enters with the newly knighted Sir Galahad and presents him to the king. The old man leads Galahad to the Siege Perilous and seats him there. The inscription on the table instantly changes to "Galahad." Moreover, all the candles suddenly blow out and thunder rumbles. The Holy Grail appears in a ray of light, hovering over the assemblage. After the wondrous experience ends, the only logical thing to do was to quest for the Holy Grail. So, they did.

Chapter 17
Lancelot's Grail

I'd heard of wonders associated with modern-day saints like Catholic mystic Therese Neumann, and gurus like Mahavatar Babaji. So when I saw those PBS shows tying a volcanic eruption to the onset of the Dark Ages, and the phenomena that occurred after Sir Lancelot became a hermit monk, I was intrigued. The idea for *Lancelot's Grail* was born.

Throughout the 1970s and into the early 1980s, Western countries experienced an influx of Indian swamis and gurus, Tibetan lamas and rinpoches, and Taoist and Zen monks. This flowering of New Age spirituality also brought Christian mystics, Kabbalistic rabbis, and Sufis into the mainstream. I attended lectures, seminars, and retreats led by many of these figures, and I had the good fortune of experiencing firsthand encounters with several individuals whom I consider fully enlightened beings.

What does that mean, "enlightened?" Worldwide, most spiritual traditions have some common threads:

- A state exists "above" our everyday mode of awareness. In that state, pure consciousness exists and can be attained. For instance, Abrahamic religions refer to Heaven and Buddhist religions refer to Nirvana.
- From that state, a creative, sustaining, conscious energy flows into us and our world.

- For certain individuals who are "seated" in this higher state of consciousness, observable quanta of spiritual energy begin to flow through and out of them. Christian examples include Jesus feeling energy flow into a woman who touched the hem of his robe, and later the Pentecost, when Jesus's disciples experienced the Holy Spirit descend into them.

Individuals through whom this conscious-energy can flow out are called saints. I define those who have risen to higher consciousness and remain seated there, as being enlightened. Whether Lancelot ever became enlightened is up for debate. In my story, he at least touches enlightenment.

Among the sheer number of New Age teachers that arose in the 70s and 80s, a certain percentage had feet of clay. Their churches and ashrams suffered sexual scandal, and their popularity either dissolved or dwindled. Didn't scandal also drive Guinevere to a nunnery and Lancelot into a hermitage?

As I watched the PBS shows, the ideas surrounding the fall of Camelot, the fall of Lancelot, and diminished sunlight initiating the Dark Ages, coalesced in my head.

I conceived of Lancelot as a man who in his time was as famous as any professional athlete of today, caught in a scandal that topples a government. Add an agrarian culture steeped in superstition and suffering the fearful loss of the sun and crops; they would surely seek someone to blame. Suddenly, with King Arthur's death, whatever advances in civilization his utopian Camelot had brought to Britain were gone. It wouldn't be difficult to imagine that the combined losses would be seen as a curse.

The entire story unfolded in my mind in one sitting—at least the bare bones of it. I knew Lancelot would be an enlightened being living in isolation, scorned and abandoned by his once-adoring public. My protagonist, Frith, a young man desperate to change his situation, would seek out Lancelot. His sister, Alura, would complicate Lancelot's life by

Chapter 17 Lancelot's Grail

romantically pursuing him. And Lancelot, uncertain of his obligation to share what he has found, just wants to be left alone.

Until I watched the Camelot documentary, I'd been ignorant of events after Camelot fell. In many modern tellings, Arthur's death is the end of the story. I raced to the library and checked out *Le Morte d'Arthur*. Later, I bought my own copy. It's not a quick read. The edition I have weighs in just shy of six hundred pages.

The first thing I learned was that Malory's version strongly emphasizes a spiritual quest that modern novelists downplay or omit, even though they use Malory as their source material. Movies and modern interpretations of the story focus on love and war, leaving us ignorant of Malory's major theme. Even Tennyson's *Idylls of the King* essentially retells Malory's stories as romance.

In further research, I read the books by Geoffrey of Monmouth and Chrétien de Troyes. I also listened to several audio and video college courses on the period and the subject matter. In the end, I relied principally on Malory, as so many other authors have—but unlike them, I retained his characters' quest for spiritual achievement. To me, this was the driving force in the knights' lives once the Grail appeared at Arthur's court.

Malory wrote about several things that resonated with reports in our own times. Malory says Lancelot lived the last months of his life without eating. Similarly, Percival encounters the Fisher King, who abstains from food, except for communion. Sound impossible? Consider Catholic nun, Sister Therese Neumann, who from 1922 until her death in 1962 ate only a daily Eucharist wafer yet remained hale and fit.

As I read, I noticed how closely Malory's descriptions of the Holy Grail's appearance paralleled the observations of New Age sojourners experiencing the higher chakras: "In a ray of light appeared the Grail, hovering. It was veiled, but every knight, damsel, king and queen in the room felt its wonder. Without even touching it, each person was elevated by its presence, according to their own nature." Anyone who has read theosophical or yogic descriptions of experiencing or being in

Figure 17-1 The Holy Grail, hidden under white silk, appearing at King Arthur's Pentecost feast. Illustrator: William Henry Margetson.

the presence of the spiritual eye recognizes that Malory's Holy Grail is not the jewel-encrusted object sought by Indiana Jones, but a portal to higher consciousness within us.

During the Arthurian knights' quest for the Grail, Lancelot had at least three significant encounters with it. According to Malory, Lancelot began to exhibit phenomena that are often ascribed to saints and ancient yogis once he became a hermit. From this, my novel postulates that in his solitude, Lancelot must have finally attained the Holy Grail.

Did Lancelot become a saint? That's certainly the way my protagonists, Frith and Alura, see him. If we have not previously seen Lancelot that way, it is because writers over the last five hundred years have omitted the spiritual aspects of Malory's text in favor of sword fights and romance. The miracles I attribute to Lancelot in my novel can all be found in *Le Morte d'Arthur*.

Admittedly, *Le Morte d'Arthur* isn't reliable history, and Malory tended to throw in everything he came across. But his descriptions of encounters with higher states of consciousness and the spiritual powers manifested by certain saints correspond to similar elements of every major world religion. His passages resonated with my memories of people I met in the 1970s whom I consider to be enlightened. I've found that there *are* people whose spiritual energy can be tangibly felt, and some could cause that energy to flow upward within me just by their proximity.

According to Malory, Lancelot was a great knight who spent the later part of his career pursuing the Holy Grail. Was it plausible that he found it after losing everything and taking up a life of meditation and solitude? I thought so. The question for my story was not whether he attained enlightenment, but whether he would share this knowledge—and if so, with whom?

Enter Frith and Alura. Based on my interactions with the high beings I had met, I tried to imagine what Lancelot would say to bring Frith and Alura along, and I imagined his reactions to their successes and failures. My Lancelot is not perfect. He has never taught about enlightenment before. He makes it up as he goes and constantly questions whether he is being effective or too indulgent with his pupils.

His past reputation resurfaces, too. I took a note from the numerous disgraced gurus and evangelical preachers who lost their flocks back in the 1970s over accusations of sexual dalliances. Alura falls in love with her spiritual teacher, and angry villagers and distraught monastics are quick to assume Lancelot, the adulterer, has returned to his old ways.

Chapter 18
Sir Bedivere

Storytelling has been used throughout history as a device to convey spiritual or inspirational teachings. Certainly, I had a head full of ideas I'd learned from the gurus I'd hung out with. I knew that once my novel's plot basics were underway, a great deal of the book would involve dialogue between Lancelot, Frith, and Alura.

In my story, Lancelot endeavors to show the siblings that their higher consciousness is ever present, but hidden behind a veil, like the covered Grail that hovered over King Arthur's feast.

When they were children, Frith and Alura had been sent by their family to live at a wealthy abbey after the sun dimmed, and food grew scarce. Unfortunately for them, no one from the family came to take them back once the sun burned brightly again, and the crops returned. After living in the abbey for ten years, they feel abandoned and, not having joined the monastic order, are desperate to get out.

Almost every scene in my novel takes place within the abbey grounds or at the small cottage in a nearby wood where Lancelot resides in solitude. Notable Arthurian characters such as Guinevere and Percival only appear in the stories Lancelot tells Frith and Alura. The exception is Sir Bedivere. His name is perhaps unfamiliar to some readers, but he long served as King Arthur's right hand, and was one of the first knights to join the fellowship of the Round Table. The bulk of my story's action is limited to Alura and Frith listening with admiring wonder at their once

Chapter 18 Sir Bedivere

famous hero's allegory of the Holy Grail, yet the book needed an antagonist. Sir Bedivere suited that role and sparked the inciting incident to get things rolling.

Figure 18-1 Sir Bedivere returns King Arthur's sword, Excalibur, to the lake. Illustrator: Walter Crane.

Sir Bedivere had been ever loyal to the king and queen. In fact, it was Bedivere who accompanied Guinevere on her journey to marry Arthur. He fought alongside Arthur in many battles, including Camlann. Bedivere sacrificed greatly, even losing a hand in one battle. He was the knight a dying Arthur entrusted to return his sword, Excalibur, to the Lady of the Lake (mentioned in Chapter 10).

After Arthur's death, Camelot fell—or fell apart. Knights of the Round Table drifted away, returning to their own fiefdoms. I imagined that Camelot's collapse and the eventual disintegration of its chivalrous ideals would not sit well with Bedivere. The aging knight had been with Arthur since the beginning of his reign.

In my story, Bedivere is a man at loose ends, nostalgic for the Camelot that once was. But he's no fool. He sees what's needed is a charismatic figure around whom the knights will rally, one whose skill as a knight is beyond question. To his mind, no one but Lancelot would do. Sure, there was that bit of scandal . . . but he believes worthy knights will recall Lancelot's prowess and forgive his transgression.

Lancelot's Grail begins with Sir Bedivere arriving at the abbey and inquiring about the whereabouts of a certain hermit. Of course, the abbot knows Lancelot's true identity and the hidden location of his hermitage in the forest, but heretofore, Alura and Frith had not.

Superstitious villagers warned boys not to play in those woods, even on a dare, saying the hermit was cursed. Many blamed him for the state of things after Camelot's fall. People of good sense avoided the recluse who slipped like a wraith in and out of early Mass in the morning fog.

It is not until Frith is called to the abbot's office and ordered to show Bedivere the way to Lancelot's cottage that Frith learns the greatest knight has been living so near. At Lancelot's hermitage, Frith listens as Bedivere presents his plan to use Lancelot as a figurehead for resurrecting the Round Table. Lancelot rejects the idea outright. Pressed by Bedivere, Lancelot finally reveals that he has found the Holy Grail and tries to show Bedivere how he, too, can attain enlightenment.

Bedivere doesn't get it but insists that if it's true, Lancelot has an obligation to travel with him and show the Grail to the other knights. Lancelot adamantly refuses. Bedivere keeps at it until an annoyed Lancelot orders him to leave. Bedivere then suggests a compromise: if he can prove there are knights willing to follow Lancelot, then Lancelot should reconsider. This provides a reason for Bedivere to reappear throughout the book.

After Bedivere departs, Frith, hoping Lancelot will make him a knight, returns to the cottage and begs Lancelot to teach him. Alura convinces Frith to let her accompany him to Lancelot's, secretly hoping to snare herself a husband.

Lancelot, torn between a desire to be left alone and an obligation to pass on his knowledge, agrees to teach them. But he soon realizes that everyone simply wants to use him. Yet, seeing the spark of awareness growing in Alura and Frith, he persists and leads them on a quest to penetrate the barriers in themselves that keep them from attaining the Grail.

Lancelot, who has been isolated for too long, finds himself enjoying their company. Over the course of their training, he interweaves his

Chapter 18 Sir Bedivere

experiences with Guinevere and Galahad, and tells of Percival meeting the Fisher King.

On one of Bedivere's last visits to the abbey, he vows that if his attempt to reorganize the Round Table fails, he will return and take up monastic life. I included this bit of foreshadowing in my novel because, according to *Le Morte d'Arthur*, after Lancelot's death, Bedivere joins a monastery and eventually rises to the position of Bishop.

Chapter 19

Percival

Percival's encounter with the Fisher King is possibly the most heavily symbolic episode in *Le Morte d'Arthur*. Unlike Galahad's fantastic achievements, which Malory presents at face value, Percival's quest is weighted with symbolism. From Galahad's first encounter with the Holy Grail, through his evolution as a miracle worker, concluding in a death scene where Jesus appears in person to take Galahad's spirit beyond, everything is presented as being literal. By contrast, everything in Percival's story is metaphorical.

Both men are young and newly knighted. But Galahad is blessed from the beginning, as evidenced in the story of the Siege Perilous. Following the Holy Grail's first appearance at court, Arthur's knights set out to quest for it. Galahad goes with them, although he has already attained it by being the only person at the feast who sees through the veil covering the Grail and thus perceives its true nature. Percival acts more in character with his youth. He is inexperienced and unsure of himself, yet also prideful and worried about keeping up a good front.

Small groups of knights are sent to quest in different directions. Percival becomes separated from his party and enters unfamiliar territory. Initially, he rides through a meadowland, but it eventually turns into a desolate wasteland and he can't find his way back. He has no choice but to keep riding. Percival wanders for a long time until he finally comes to a mighty river. He follows its banks but finds nowhere to ford. It is nearing dusk when he finally spies three men in a small fishing boat.

Chapter 19 Percival

Percival hails them, but they are anchored far out in the current. This makes it necessary to converse by shouting across the water. Percival calls out, "Can you tell me where there is a bridge, or at least a ford?"

"Not for twenty leagues in either direction," one of them shouts back. "No ferry, either—not one that can carry a knight and his horse."

Now, Percival, still new to the trials of the quest, is losing hope. He knows there is nothing behind him. On the boat, the eldest fisherman lies upon a litter covered with fine cloth, instructing his son on where to cast the nets. The old man takes measure of Percival and offers to lodge him for the night, giving him directions to his dwelling.

Percival, glad for the invitation, follows the old man's instructions and rides off at once. But his elation soon dissipates. For when he reaches the top of the hill and looks out, there is no cottage, no house—not even a tiny hut. He decides the fishermen had made a sport of his situation and tricked him into riding away. He curses them for their practical joke.

Then, at the far end of the valley, he spies the top of a tower. He rides down into the valley and along its hollow. As he draws nearer to the distant tower, he sees that it has turrets and is a substantial castle, hardly the humble fisherman's cottage he'd anticipated. He regrets his bad thoughts about the men and repents deeply. As he is about to learn, the old fisherman is, in fact, ruler of this land, known to his people as the Fisher King.

When Percival approaches the castle, he sees the drawbridge is already lowered. He crosses the bridge and finds that his arrival is expected. Attendants come to greet him. One takes his horse; another helps him remove his armor and takes charge of it. Others lead him to his rooms. Percival reposes in his rooms until two attendants come for him.

Percival travels light at this point in his life, without retinue or even a change of clothes. With his armor removed, he is rather shabby and dirty from the road. The attendants take note that he is ill prepared to be received at court. So they bring him basins of water, and once he

Figure 19-1 Percival arrives at the Fisher King's castle.

washes, another attendant brings him a splendid robe. The robe is made of fine wool and beautifully embroidered, the sort of thing a royal would wear. He is given to know that it has been loaned to him by the mistress of the castle herself.

Thus attired, he is led into the great hall. When he has been seated, there enters an assembly of knights bearing the crippled king on a litter. They help the king onto a luxurious couch near Percival. The king is much beloved by the people in his domain, like a father. He wears a crown of sable and a robe of the same rich fur. He speaks graciously to Percival, "Please take no offense if I do not rise to greet you, for I can move only with great pain."

Tables are brought in and set before them. They enter into good conversation, and there is much feasting, but the king does not partake of the food.

During the celebration, a wondrous pageant ensues. A procession enters the hall, each bearer carrying a mystical object. The first, a youth, carries a white lance, the tip of which emits drops of blood that run down it. Next come two squires carrying a golden candelabra with ten branches that fill the chamber with light. Thereafter follows the queen, bearing a grail from which streams such a brilliant light that the candles—which, only moments before, had illuminated the chamber—are now overcome just as the moon and stars are by the morning sun. The grail is wide and

Chapter 19 Percival

somewhat deep, large enough to serve a pike or a salmon, but it contains only a bit of bread—the Eucharist.

When the king sees it, he bows before it, saying, "Mea culpa." All those present do the same. Although the church forbade women from acting in a priestly capacity, the queen serves the Eucharist, the king receives it, and no one present objects. Percival then learns that the Fisher King survives on only one small wafer of Holy bread a day.

Percival does not comprehend the mysteries of the pageant he's just seen. He burns to ask their meaning, but is afraid doing so will show his ignorance. His embarrassment keeps him silent.

In fact, he is having his first encounter with the Holy Grail. The Grail appears again and again as each course is served, completely uncovered so that he might see its nature. But Percival does not inquire about it. If he had, he would have achieved the Grail experience himself, then and there. Instead, he tells himself that he will definitely ask someone in the morning when he's ready to leave, when the revelation of his ignorance will no longer matter. So he keeps eating.

Percival's failure becomes apparent to the king, and it makes him very sad. He says to Percival, "If you don't mind, I must go to my bed. Please stay in the hall as long as you wish." Four stout knights come and carry the king away.

After the king's departure, Percival continues to puzzle over all the things he'd been shown. The lance that bled and the grail to which the king and all his kin had bowed are beyond his understanding. Trying to figure it out makes him very weary. He retires and sleeps soundly until morning.

When he arises, he dresses and goes down to the court. He looks in the yard and in the great hall but finds no one. The empty castle fills him with sorrow. Fully intending to ask about all he'd witnessed the previous night, he comes upon nary a soul. However, he finds his armor laid out for him and his horse in the livery already fed, saddled, and ready to go.

With no other recourse at hand, he puts on his armor and mounts his horse. He is surprised to find the castle gate open and the drawbridge already lowered for him. He thinks that perhaps the people have gone into the fields and he'll find them there. As he crosses over, the drawbridge begins to rise while he's still on it. His horse has to jump the last few feet in open air. He looks back to see the castle is now sealed against him.

He rides through the valley without finding the castle's occupants. He thinks that perhaps they are in the woods, harvesting nuts or fruits, or gathering wood. He turns from the valley meadows into the forest but rides until evening without finding a man or woman whom he can ask. Later, Percival comes to understand that if he'd asked the appropriate question, he would've healed the king and his kingdom.

Percival does eventually find the Grail, but he missed his best opportunity and had to quest for many more years before attaining it.

Percival's story has been retold many times over the centuries, notably by Chrétien de Troyes, whose untimely death stopped the story mid-sentence. Robert de Boron continued Chrétien's *Percival*, and four other continuations were written by the thirteenth-century French poet Gerbert de Montreuil. In the same period, Wolfram von Eschenbach created a German version titled *Parzival*. Later, Sir Thomas Malory folded Percival into *Le Morte d'Arthur*.

Details differ in each author's version, but they all agree on the purpose to be achieved and the effect of Percival's success or failure. For example, in Gerbert's continuation, Percival does not ask the right question of the Fisher King because he feels himself a sinner, unfit to know the truth about the Grail. In the version I presented in this chapter, which I adapted from Malory, Percival fails to ask because he is self-conscious about how he will look to others.

Percival's story of meeting the Fisher King is filled with hidden meaning. Every phase of the wondrous feast at the castle brings forth sacred symbols. Percival was shown the Grail again and again, yet his mind

Chapter 19 Percival

dwells on the shallow and unimportant. So it goes for many people as they make their first forays on the path to enlightenment.

Even the Fisher King himself is a Christian allegory. When Percival meets the king, the king's men are casting nets on the water. The king is like a father to his whole kingdom. It is his responsibility to guide the people on a spiritual path to their own realization. Their souls are drowning. Using the net, he tries to draw them into his boat. But the king's health is failing. No longer able to throw the net himself, he has to keep instructing the men on where to throw it. They don't get it on their own. When Percival arrives, the king hopes he's found a spiritual successor—one whom he can make understand that it is the enlightened man's duty to draw men into realization. But Percival isn't ready.

In *Lancelot's Grail*, Lancelot tells Frith and Alura the story of Percival meeting the Fisher King twice. The first time, he tells the story to calm Frith and Alura's concerns after they discover he no longer eats anything other than the bit of bread and wine served at communion.

Later in the novel, Lancelot has a premonition that he doesn't have long to complete their training. He ramps up his efforts to bring them to self-realization and things go awry.

In Lancelot's opinion, Percival isn't entirely at fault; the Fisher King had pushed him too hard, forcing him to see things he wasn't ready to understand. Lancelot fears he has made the Fisher King's mistake with Frith and Alura and tells them the second part of Percival's story as an apology for failing them. They don't comprehend it any better than Percival did, and each sibling thinks Lancelot is comparing their lack of progress to Percival's. Lancelot disabuses them of this notion, explaining what he actually means.

For those who haven't read Malory and wonder what question Percival *should* have asked, the question is, "Whom does the Grail serve?"

Chapter 20
LANCELOT'S DISCIPLE

The influx of mystical knowledge of other cultures from the 1970s through the present day helps Westerners understand concepts of which preceding American and European cultures were unaware. In my novel, Lancelot serves that same function by explaining New Age spirituality to characters of an earlier time. The problem I faced telling the story was vocabulary.

I don't mean choosing between using Old English or Modern English to tell the story. A glance at a version of Chaucer that includes the text in its original Middle English on the left, with the Modern English transliteration on the facing page, answered that question before I even wrote the first word. Even peppering the story with bits of Old English would have made it inscrutable to the average reader, and I wanted the reader's attention to be on what Lancelot was saying—not struggling to puzzle out Old English.

I wrote *Lancelot's Grail* in Modern English, but the "voice" of the text gave it a sense of a period long ago by being a little stiff—minimal use of contractions and no slang whatsoever. Still, I needed substitute terms for Sanskrit words that have become part of our twentieth-century vocabulary. For example, the average person today would at least vaguely recognize the words "yoga" or "karma." Perhaps some readers would also know chakra, prana, or Shakti. But all of those words would be out of place in a story set in a sixth-century British abbey.

Chapter 20 Lancelot's Disciple

Outside of English, Latin was the only other language true to the period and setting. Previous Roman occupancy had made it the de facto standard for church records, as well as legal and religious texts. Boys were taught to read and write Latin as their primary form of literacy, and Lancelot certainly would have learned it in his youth. So, I began looking for Latin equivalents to use in place of Sanskrit terms.

Shakti is a key concept I had learned from Indian swamis and gurus, for which I needed to find a substitute word. In the simplest definition, Shakti is divine power or energy. In the personal sense, it is the energy force that moves through us, and keeps us alive. In yogic philosophy, Shakti is closely linked with (but not identical to) *prana*, which is more specifically the life force that courses within us causing our diaphragms to move and making us breathe. The actual scope of prana is a little broader than that. While it's said to permeate all levels of reality, "prana" is the Sanskrit word for breath. When I searched for Latin synonym, *spiritus* seemed very close. It translates as breath, soul, or life. I thought it could stand in for prana, but it didn't seem quite sufficient for Shakti.

Then, I came across *energia*, which the Romans derived from the Greek *enérgeia*, one definition of which is "supernatural action or cosmic force." Ah, that was the one. It didn't hurt that the spelling was visually similar to "energy" so that readers would subconsciously think of that word every time they saw it.

Even after finding the right vocabulary substitutions, it was challenging to write a novel in which a character explains New Age metaphysical ideas using examples and language true to the Dark Ages. At least Hermann Hesse had the good sense to set his novella, *Siddhartha,* in India, where discussions of yoga fit naturally.

I don't recall which draft of *Lancelot's Grail* I was working on when the idea for a sequel came to me, but it was long after my return from Britain when I began conceptualizing it.

I had already completed numerous revisions to *Lancelot's Grail*. Ernest Hemingway's famous quote, "Writing is rewriting" rings true for most authors, and I had many more rewrites in my future before *Lancelot's*

Grail would be published. Still, I paused my revision process to make a quick synopsis of story ideas the sequel would cover, and then I put it aside while *Lancelot's Grail* went through the steps of editing, proofreading, publication, and marketing.

By the time the book came out, I was weary of the constraints of writing about 550 CE, so I wrote an unrelated novel that takes place in the early twentieth century. When that was finished, and I was ready to return to Frith and Alura, I knew Frith needed to get out of the abbey—and I did, too.

To expand on the topics introduced in *Lancelot's Grail*, I needed to move the story outside the confines of Britain to a region where people used foreign words naturally. I decided my protagonist would journey to a land where men conversed about higher realms using the metaphysical words that the flowering of New Age spirituality had made familiar to today's reader.

In my original notes for a sequel, Frith's travel abroad was only backstory in the plot, but as I set about developing the novel, his journey on the Silk Road became the core of *Lancelot's Disciple*.

From research, I learned that the Silk Road had conveyed much more than silk. The caravans and merchants spread new ideas and religions as they went. In fact, that is how Buddhism spread from India to China, and how many other religious philosophies spread through the Mideast. Of course, my characters could never travel into India or China. The time period of my sequel is 554 CE, about 700 years before China would allow the first Westerner admittance—Marco Polo.

For centuries, silk, spices, and luxury goods moved overland, from China through India, and then into the Mideast through territories that are now Afghanistan and Uzbekistan. From there, camel caravans transported goods on a long arduous trek over thousands of miles of desert to the Mediterranean Sea where ships bound for Rome, Gaul, Britain and elsewhere took over.

Chapter 20 Lancelot's Disciple

The land portion of the route crossed all the Mideast and Central Asian territories between Afghanistan and modern day Syria and Lebanon. The powerful Sassanians controlled it, kept the trade routes open, and protected the caravans. The Sassanian king had a palace just outside Baghdad, but Samarkand was the trade's Central Asian capital, located at the foot of the Pamir Mountains in what is today Uzbekistan.

The first plot requirement for my sequel was to get Frith out of the abbey. I invented a Jewish merchant, Jacob, who for many years had been a business partner of Frith and Alura's wealthy father. Their father charges Jacob with teaching Frith the merchant vocation. Jacob plans a journey to purchase silk in the Mideast and arrives at the abbey to take Frith with him.

The trip involves sailing from Britain to Italy, crossing the Mediterranean to Egypt, and then following the coast to Tyre, a city on the edge of the Arabian desert where Jacob has a warehouse. Jacob has made this trip frequently, but this time he intends to organize a camel caravan and travel inland where silk prices are lower.

Figure 20-1 The route Frith and Jacob travel by sea.

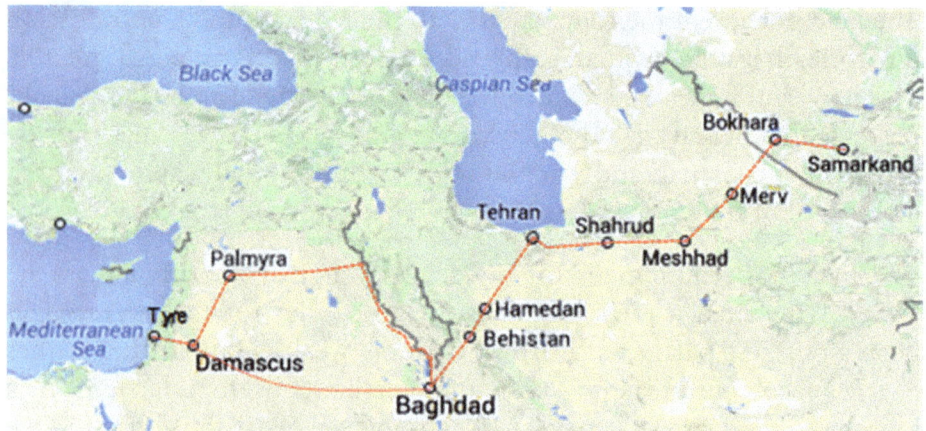

Figure 20-2 The route traveled by Frith and Jacob by camel.

Over the course of the caravan journey, Jacob presses farther east, seeking ever lower prices, eventually winding up in Samarkand. At the time, Samarkand was not only the Sassanian trade capital but also the point where silk and luxury items from China and India were transferred to Mideast caravans. It was a city where foreigners of very different cultures intermingled and exchanged ideas.

In *Lancelot's Grail*, Lancelot taught Frith and Alura to perceive a separation between the observer and the observed, and also how to use *energia* to pierce the veil hiding the Grail. But Lancelot's teachings are based only on his own encounters with the Grail.

I had met Christian mystics, Buddhist lamas, Kabbalistic rabbis, swamis and gurus, and I wanted to go beyond what Lancelot experienced to bring some of their ideas into the sequel.

One almost universal teaching these men and women had in common was the advice to get beyond pride. Yet, I frequently observed that wealthy people hanging around them seemed to count saints among their possessions. So I added a character, the Sultan, who possessed an attituded similar to the wealthy people I'd observed.

In Samarkand, Jacob's caravan must wait for the next shipment of silk to arrive from India. While waiting, Jacob and Frith meet the Sultan, a wealthy collector of Oriental holy men. Staying at his palace, are a

Chapter 20 Lancelot's Disciple

Taoist monk, a Buddhist monk, and a Hindu swami. Frith and Jacob are invited to stay as well. This sets the stage for dialogues between the Sultan's guests, in which they discuss similarities among their disparate religions.

Unlike for *Lancelot's Grail*, where I visited Britain to gather details about the setting, traveling to authentic lands wasn't possible for *Lancelot's Disciple*. Today, the countries Jacob's caravan crossed are either at war or hostile to Americans. So I relied on documentary and travel DVDs to see what the landscape looks like in various locations where the story takes place. Fortunately, I have a friend who had actually been to Samarkand and he read my descriptions for accuracy. I also met someone who had ridden camels, and who gave me a good sense of that experience. Furthermore, portions of Frith's journey involve travel through Britain's countryside—both when he leaves to reach the ship and when he returns to the abbey. For these portions, I relied on the photos and notes from my trip to Britain.

No author I've ever heard of writes a novel in one pass—certainly not me. As with *Lancelot's Grail*, *Lancelot's Disciple* required many revisions. From my first draft through final editing and proofreading, the book took three years to write and publish. I knew it had been worth the effort when a local synagogue's book club bought ten copies to study and discuss in-depth. I felt I'd succeeded in crafting a fictional story that communicated esoteric ideas.

Chapter 21
Photographic References

Had my journey through Britain traipsing around places associated with King Arthur been worthwhile? Absolutely.

Although both *Lancelot's Grail* and *Lancelot's Disciple* are novels, they are chock full of ideas—describing meditation techniques and comparing world religions and New Age philosophies. To bear such a weighty subtext, a story set in Arthurian times must be believable. It may seem like a contradiction, but one method of making fiction engaging is to root it in reality. Incorporating seemingly insignificant details I discovered on my trip added authenticity in subtle ways.

Fiction writers can make up whatever world they want. But for the reader to accept the big picture, the underlying details need to be accurate, especially about things the reader might know. The classic example of inauthenticity is the old-time Western TV shows where the hero's six gun fires ten or fifteen shots without reloading.

Creating a novel that facilitated suspension of disbelief was especially important to me because I wanted readers to focus on what Alura and Frith were being told, rather than being sidetracked by inaccurate descriptions. Beyond simply being genuine, details such as the layout of the abbey kitchen or a community cider press settle the reader into the Arthurian world.

I returned from Britain with 740 photographs that refreshed my memory as I wrote descriptive paragraphs of the settings in *Lancelot's Grail*.

Chapter 21 Photographic References

And for *Lancelot's Disciple* I relied on photos and videos gathered from the Internet. To illustrate the ways in which these visual references informed my writing, I'll share brief passages from the novels alongside the photos I used for their inspiration. Some of these passages illustrate tiny details whereas others represent major settings.

The most important of these settings was the abbey. During my trip to England, I visited the ruins of Glastonbury Abbey, which I used as the model for my fictional monastery. Here is an excerpt from Lancelot's Grail in which I drew detail from my visit:

> Frith crossed to the main building which held the cloister, scriptorium, library, and the Abbot's office. A breeze danced up his sleeves, tickling the newly minted man-hair under his arms. The carefree summer day made him feel as exuberant as a young colt. His work was done and soon Alura's would be too.
>
> He made his way through the library. The room consisted of wooden cupboards filled with books. The Abbot had told him it was one of the largest in the land, containing more than just religious books, but also books on natural history, politics and the law.
>
> He passed into the scriptorium, where generations of monks had sat huddled in carrels, producing page after page of velum covered with ink. A few of the monks were illuminating the manuscripts with colorful illustrations. Frith quite liked those, but the rest meant little to him, for he could not read. He liked the scriptorium though— it was the brightest, sunniest room in the abbey.
>
> Leaving the scriptorium, he passed through a small, ledger-filled room where the abbey kept its records. Adjacent to it was the Abbot's office.

Figure 21-1 Pigs on spits in a tall fireplace at the Abbot's Kitchen.

Chapter 21 Photographic References

My experience at Glastonbury Abbey informed scenes for both *Lancelot's Grail* and *Lancelot's Disciple*. My tour of the reconstructed Abbot's kitchen formed the basis for my description of Alura's workplace. I learned that women were employed even at all-male monasteries, and I also saw how the kitchen's architectural design supplied a draft to the fireplaces. Here is a description of the kitchen that I wrote for *Lancelot's Grail*, which incorporates this knowledge.

> Alura and Frith entered the Abbot's kitchen. Its tall, conical ceiling, open at the top, provided a draft that kept three fireplaces blazing.

I also describe the kitchen in *Lancelot's Disciple* using details I gathered from my visit to Glastonbury Abbey.

> The Abbot's kitchen was Frith's favorite place, and not only because Alura worked there. It was always full of savory aromas—venison or boar roasting on one fireplace, a chicken or a goose on another, and a great pot of vegetables on the third.

Even though much has changed in the 1500 years since Arthur's time, walking the land and visiting sites of Arthurian legend created lingering impressions in my mind that came through in my writing.

While climbing the Glastonbury Tor for instance, I walked along a path that was separated from a forest by a dense hedge of berries that must have been a mile long. Although the photo I took during that walk seems insignificant, I referenced the image in both novels when I described my characters penetrating just such a hedge to enter the woods where Lancelot's hermitage is located.

Figure 21-2 A thick hedge of berries.

In the following scene from *Lancelot's Grail*, Frith and Alura pick a basket of ripe berries there:

> When they reached the thorny bushes, Frith noticed many of them still had good berries, but scolded himself— This was no time to think about food. They followed the hedge along until Frith found an opening. Though the hedge still appeared impenetrable, Frith easily slipped between two bushes and led them into the dense woods.
>
> ———
>
> She [Alura] carried a basket on one arm. "We're going to pick the blackberries that you said grow at the edge of the woods."
>
> "No, we're not."
>
> "You, my young brother, are allowed to go where you will.

CHAPTER 21 PHOTOGRAPHIC REFERENCES

I may be asked to account for myself. Therefore, my pretense is that we have gone for berries."

Frith was keen to get to Lancelot's, but when they reached the hedge, she insisted he wait while she picked some berries. "I'm as eager to see this great knight as you, but I shouldn't return with an empty basket, should I?"

In addition to describing the path and the berry bushes on the way to Lancelot's hermitage, I described wattle in my novels—the material that both his fence and cottage were made from. I learned a lot about wattle during my trip. For example, the first Christian church in Britain was originally constructed of wattle and mud. It was also used for fencing. On my hike to the site of Camelot I came across a wattle fence and photographed it. Later, I used it as the inspiration for the wattle fence around Lancelot's garden; additionally I described his cottage as being made from wattle and mud, as a building in the Dark Ages might have been.

Figure 21-3 A fence made from wattle.

161

Quest for Lancelot's Arthur

Here is a description from *Lancelot's Grail*:

> Lancelot's cottage was separated from the forest by a rough wattle fence. In Bedivere's opinion it was a poor fence. . . . Beyond the gardens was a cottage—though cottage would be a generous term for it. It was poorly thatched and barely large enough for a man.
>
> Bedivere looked at the shack; looked at Lancelot's poor dress. "The grace of God is treating you pretty shabbily, then. Your cottage is little more than wattle and mud. You deserve better."

Unlike many of the scenes and settings in *Lancelot's Grail*, I had to find inspiration outside of my own experience for *Lancelot's Disciple* because the characters travel the Silk Road by camel caravan—something I'd never done. To portray this experience, I first had to learn the difference between two camel species. The dromedary, the type we are most familiar with today, was not used on the Silk Road. Instead, caravans used

Figure 21-4 On right, dromedary camel. Photo: John O'Neill.‡ On left, Bactrain camels such as those used on the Silk Road. Photo: Yaan.‡

Chapter 21 Photographic References

the Bactrian, which was native to Central Asia. The Bactrian is larger and has two humps. Although I've ridden an elephant, I've never been on a camel. Fortunately, I met someone who had been, and based on his description I was able to write a funny scene conveying Frith's first experience:

> Frith timidly reached out and patted his camel's muscular neck. The hair was long and thick—more like stroking a carpet than a horse. The Bedouin nodded his approval. Frith threw his right leg over the camel's back and pulled himself on. The Bedouin handed Frith the reins and tapped the camel's shoulder. The camel stretched his neck forward and came up on his front knees. Frith canted backwards, holding onto the reins for his life. Then the beast raised its rear haunches, slamming Frith forward. He grabbed for the camel's neck. The animal straightened its front legs, throwing Frith rearward again. Once he recovered, Frith found himself higher than he'd ever been, able to see over the roofs of the squat houses nearby.

A critical requirement of historical fiction is avoiding anachronisms—elements more recent than the time period in which the story takes place. In the case of *Lancelot's Disciple*, the characters traverse the Silk Road in 554 AD, but nearly all my reference photos of cities along the route included mosques with minarets. Unfortunately, the Prophet Muhammad didn't found Islam until almost a century later, so it would have been anachronistic to include them in my novel's landscape.

Samarkand was the capital of the Silk Road trade, and where my characters spent time there awaiting the next shipment of silk. The skyline of present-day Samarkand bears Islamic influence on its architecture. When I described the city in *Lancelot's Disciple*, I was sure to avoid referencing this type of architecture, but mentioned the Pamir Mountains behind the city:

Figure 21-5 Modern-day Samarkand. Photo: Gilad Rom.‡

> Samarkand itself was a fortified city at the base of ancient mountains standing in the distance. They [Jacob's caravan] entered the gates and located the place caravans camped, on the city's eastern boundary where the Zarafshon River flowed. Thick vegetation, flowers, and fruits were plentiful along the river. What a welcome change from the desert.

After having transcendental experiences with the holy men in Samarkand, Frith has a lot to sort out. Once he returns to Britain, he goes on a long walkabout while trying to reconcile with the everyday world. He rests one day among mossy boulders on the Bodmin Moor similar to the ones in my reference photograph in Figure 21-6.

CHAPTER 21 PHOTOGRAPHIC REFERENCES

Figure 21-6 Mossy woods similar to the place where Frith rested. Photo: Helen Hotson.†

It was near noon by the time the fog lifted. By then, he'd [Frith] reached a forest strewn with mossy boulders. No path here, but that was all right. He sat down on a lichen-covered rock and searched his bag for one of the round loaves he'd thought to bring.

He looked about him and realized a tree was just a tree, the rock was just a rock, and moss was spongy and wet. What he preferred didn't matter a bit to any of them. Once he got his personal thoughts out of the way, Shakti could flow freely between the planes.

Raindrops began to fall around him. He stood up, brushed the damp moss from his backside and ran for the cover of a large oak.

Figure 21-7 The stone base of an ancient cider press.

During my UK travels, I photographed the stone base of a giant Medieval cider press, and so Frith, during his walkabout, also came upon an autumn cider pressing in the following scene in *Lancelot's Disciple*:

> "There's a cider press at the next crossroads, bit of a farmer's market around it. Thought I'd set out my wares and do a crumb of business. Come with me, if you want. . ."

———

> Frith wandered over to the cider press. It was a cylinder formed of precisely fitted slats held by iron bands and set into a large circular stone with a grooved lip. As the apples

Chapter 21 Photographic References

were crushed from above, sweet brown juice rushed out the lip into waiting buckets. The buckets were emptied into barrels set on the cart that brought the apples. Frith drank from a proffered ladle. The cider was sweet, with just a hint of tartness.

Years after *Lancelot's Disciple* was published, that cider press scene brought me full-circle back to Arthur. One evening, I sat on my couch sipping hard cider I'd discovered for sale at my local supermarket and bought because I'd remembered the cider press. The cider's crisp, tangy flavor reminded me of the pub I'd visited in Tintagel, which caused me to glance up at an oil painting on my living room wall. After my trip to England, my father had painted me standing in front of the ruins of Britain's Tintagel Castle. As I looked at the painting, I started to ponder what I had learned and written about King Arthur and his knights.

Chapter 22
Myths and Bliss

Although I returned from Britain convinced that Arthur was a real person, I was equally convinced that the Arthurian legends are just that: legend, not factual history. The written versions derive from an amalgam of oral histories and fireside tales from Brittany, Cornwall, Wales, and Ireland. These were repurposed for use in clerical sermons and to justify one set of values over another, depending on the need of the times.

Written tales of King Arthur, Camelot, and the Holy Grail have captivated readers for nine hundred years, and the oral versions for six hundred years before that. Why?

Joseph Campbell, unquestionably the world's leading authority on comparative mythology, believed all people in all cultures need stories to help them understand themselves. For Campbell, whether the story is fact or myth is less important than its ability to inform.

So few of our myths originated in the English-speaking world. In addition to Arthur, one might include later myths such as Beowulf and Robin Hood, but these never conveyed a meaning deeper than their basic plot. The stories of King Arthur and his knights endured because time and again, they helped people of each era understand their nature.

Stories of King Arthur's knights reflected courtly love and defined chivalry for the twelfth-century. In Sir Thomas Mallory's time, they invoked feudal fealty and fidelity to the king. A nineteenth century adaptation emphasized love and betrayal for Victorians. Twentieth-century kids,

Chapter 22 Myths and Bliss

raised on comics, movies, TV, and video games, bought into sword fights and battles. Now, New Age interests, like those found throughout today's Glastonbury, concentrate on the spiritual aspects of the Grail quest.

In my own reading, I've always appreciated the way authors as diverse as Robert Heinlein and Hermann Hesse wrote novels that conveyed spiritual concepts. In fact, storytelling has been used throughout history to impart spiritual or inspirational teachings.

Arthurian stories cover many aspects of the human experience, but none are more important than the quest for the Grail. Joseph Campbell said that the seat of the soul is where the outer world and inner worlds meet. He asserted that anyone could find bliss by following it deep inside. So, I interpreted Lancelot's period of hermitage after the fall of Camelot as his way of following his bliss to the Grail—that Grail being a state of enlightenment. The question for Lancelot, then, is what he's meant to do with it.

In *Lancelot's Disciple*, the sequel to *Lancelot's Grail*, Frith meets a monk named Buddhita who clearly emphasizes that the real purpose of attaining enlightenment is to uplift others.

In both novels, the answer of what to do with enlightenment once you attain it is to give it away. I don't pretend to be in that state myself or to know why those who are enlightened manifest spirituality as they do. But I do seek the inner state and occasionally experience bliss.

Looking at my father's painting of the fragmented walls of Tintagel, Arthur's birthplace, I thought Campbell was definitely on the right track. He said that even though civilizations crumble, mythologies prevail. I hope *Lancelot's Grail* has played a part by bringing forth an interpretation for New Age readers.

Acknowledgments

Thank you to members of Writers Alliance of Gainesville who critiqued the book as I was writing it: Susie Baxter, Joan H. Carter, Ronnie Lovler, Ann~Marie Magné; my copyeditor: Signe Jorgenson; my proofreaders: Cindy Elder and Connie Morrison. Special thanks to Ken Campbell who loaned me numerous books on King Arthur and the Arthurian period.

Photographs and Figures Credits

All photos © Richard Gartee except as noted below.

† Licensed from Adobe, Inc.

Figure 12-3 Illustrator: George Bailey

Figure 16-4 Photo: David Mathews Lyons

Figure 21-6 Photo: Helen Hotson

‡ Licensed under terms of creative commons.org:

Figure 3-2 Photo: Daderot, https://commons.wikimedia.org/w/index.php?curid=5960974

Figure 3-5 Photo: Kurt Thomas Hunt, https://commons.wikimedia.org/w/index.php?curid=101314833

Figure 9-1 Photo: Nilfanion, https://commons.wikimedia.org/w/index.php?curid=47690087

Figure 9-2 Photo: Nilfanion, https://commons.wikimedia.org/w/index.php?curid=47690249

Figure 9-3 Photo: Jim Champion, https://commons.wikimedia.org/w/index.php?curid=5073365

Figure 12-4 Illustrator: Adamsan, https://commons.wikimedia.org/w/index.php?curid=167793

Figure 13-4 Photo: Jarkeld, https://commons.wikimedia.org/w/index.php?curid=62974269

Figure 13-6 Photo: Detmar Owen, https://commons.wikimedia.org/w/index.php?curid=70228378

Figure 13-7 Photo: Dick Bauch, https://commons.wikimedia.org/wiki/File:ASC_Allee_1_db.jpg

Figure 15-1 Photo: Romary, https://commons.wikimedia.org/w/index.php?curid=2784754

Figure 15-3 Photo: Colin Cheesman, https://commons.wikimedia.org/wiki/File:Geoffrey_of_Monmouth_at_Tintern_Station_(geograph_6023609).jpg

Figure 16-5 Photo: R. S. Nourse, https://commons.wikimedia.org/wiki/File:King_Arthur's_Round_Table_at_Winchester_Castle,_Winchester,_Hampshire,_England.png

Acknowledgments

Figure 21-4 Dromedary camel photo: John O'Neill, https://commons.wikimedia.org/w/index.php?curid=2831408
Bactrain camel photo: Yaan, https://commons.wikimedia.org/w/index.php?curid=6407912

Figure 21-5 Photo: Gilad Rom, https://en.m.wikipedia.org/wiki/File:Samarkand_view_from_the_top.jpg

Images in public domain:

Figure 15-2 Engraving from illustrated manuscript, artist unknown.

Figure 15-4 Photo: Adrian Pingstone

Figure 15-5 Engraving from Bibliothèque nationale de France, 1530, artist unknown.

Figure 15-6 Etching 1516, artist unknown, The Granger Collection, New York.

Figure 16-1 Cover, Illustrator: Aubrey Beardsley (1893)

Figure 16-2 Illustrator: Atelier d'Evrard d'Espinques (1475)

Figure 16-3 Illustration from *Notice sur la vie et les écrits de Robert Wace* by Frédéric Pluquet, 1824. Engraving by C. E. Lambert.

Figure 16-6 Illustrator: Walter Crane from King *Arthur's Knights: The Tales Retold for Boys and Girls* by Henry Gilbert (1911).

Figure 17-1 Illustrator: William Henry Margetson, *Legends of King Arthur and His Knights* by Janet MacDonald Clark (E. Nister, 1914)

Figure 18-1 Illustrator: Walter Crane from King *Arthur's Knights: The Tales Retold for Boys and Girls* by Henry Gilbert (1911).

Figure 19-1 Detail from a 1330 manuscript of *Perceval ou Le Conte du Graal* by Chrétien de Troyes, artist unknown.

About the Author

Richard Gartee is an award-winning novelist who has authored eight novels, six collections of poetry, four nonfiction books, and seven college textbooks. His novels, *Lancelot's Grail* and *Lancelot's Disciple*, were researched during the trip described in this book. If you haven't read them, you are encouraged to do so.

A complete list of his available titles, upcoming events, and forthcoming books is available at www.gartee.com.

If you enjoyed this book, please take a moment to leave a short review on Amazon and/or other booksellers' websites. Reviews help to sell books, and sales help an author to keep writing. You can readily find links to other online booksellers' websites by visiting www.lepublications.com and clicking on the book cover image.

You can sign up to receive updates on new publications by this author at either site or by scanning this QR code:

www.ingramcontent.com/pod-product-compliance
Lightning Source LLC
Chambersburg PA
CBHW072015070526
44583CB00015B/1491